I0468100

Swing Trading Easiest Guide

Complete and Comprehensive Guide on How to Invest and Earn Huge Profits With the Best Swing Trading Strategies

Table of Contents

Introduction

The following chapters will discuss all the different aspects of swing trading. You will learn why swing trading is one of the most lucrative ways of trading the financial markets and making consistent profits.

This book will introduce you to swing trading and what it is all about. You will learn the basics as well as intermediate skills that all successful swing traders need to learn. These include all the different strategies, tools, software, platforms, and so much more.

By the time you finish reading this book, you will know how to read and interpret charts, where to find the best stocks to trade, and how to conduct comprehensive fundamental and financial analysis.

Chapter 1: A Basic Overview of Swing Trading

If you are a seasoned stock market trader, then you already know that there are different styles of trading stocks or other financial market instruments. One of these styles is swing trading.

Swing trading is a trading style where your main aim is to make gains in a financial instrument such as stocks over a period of time. This time period ranges from a couple of days to several weeks. This type of trading is a short-term trading style best suited for trading options and stocks.

As a swing trader, you will mostly rely on technical analysis to identify profitable trading opportunities. You can also expect to make use of fundamental analysis as well as patterns and price trends analysis.

Why Swing Trading?

The main aim of swing trading is to find the major trend and then apply swing trading strategies to the trend in order to earn profits and make big wins. As a swing trader, you will hold either a short or long position in the marketing often for a minimum of 2 days to probably 2 weeks.

This time frame is not exact because some trades conclude pretty fast, while others may last for a few months. Even in such rare instances, the strategy is still considered to be swing trade. Your aim in all instances will be to profit from large price movements.

There are some swing traders who prefer less volatile and more sedate financial instruments, while others opt for very volatile ones. In both instances, a trader will try to identify the direction of an asset's price before moving in and eventually cashing in on the profit made from the price movement. Successful swing traders aim to benefit from large chunks of the desired price movement before proceeding to the next available chance.

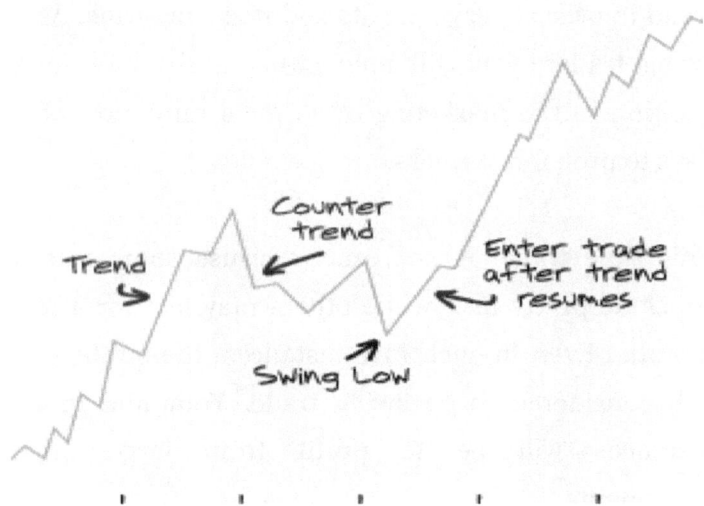

Technical Analysis

As a swing trader, you will use technical analysis just about all the time so that you can identify the trend and benefit from its movement. Most of the time, there will be neither a bearish nor bullish movement at the markets. However, sometimes a stock or other security may be moving in a trend that is predictable, especially between the support and resistance areas.

Even in this instance, there are swing trading opportunities. As a trader, you should assume a short position close to the resistance area or a long position.

Sometimes, it takes a couple of weeks or even months to benefit from an expected price movement.

It is crucial to note that swing trading can expose you to the weekend or overnight risks. What happens is that you may enter a position during the day, but then, unforeseen events take place overnight or in the course of the weekend. These events could affect the price movement and substantially affect your position in the markets.

There is an established and trusted risk versus reward ratio used by swing traders to take profits. This ratio is largely based on a profit target as well as established, pre-determined stop loss levels. The system can be set up such that profit taking happens when a certain profit level is attained or when a certain loss level is attained.

A Popular Trading Strategy

Swing trading has proven to be among the most preferred forms of trading and making money. It is important to ensure that your technical analysis skills are up to scratch if you are to trade and be profitable consistently. You will also be assessing trades based on a risk versus reward ratio. This is done using charts. Chart analysis will help you to determine where to enter a trade, when to exit and where to take profits. As a swing trader, you will mostly rely on the 15-minute or 1-hour charts to determine the most suitable stop loss and entry points.

Apart from technical analysis, you will also need to ensure that your fundamental analysis skills are up to scratch. For instance, you may notice that a stock is on an upward trend, and you want to get any benefit from its movement. Before doing so, you will need to confirm that its fundamentals are sound and secure.

As a trader, you can risk about $1 in order to make $3. This is considered a reasonable and favorable risk to reward level. However, risking $1 to make perhaps $1 or less is considered unfavorable.

Upward Trend Favored by Bullish Traders

Stock movement in the markets hardly follows a straight line. Instead, the movement forms a pattern that is step-like. As an example, a stock or other instrument might trend upwards for a couple of days then take a dip for a while before resuming its upward trend. When you closely examine these patterns for a while and observe that the entire movement keeps moving upwards, then we can declare that the stock has an upward trend.

Bullish traders need to first identify the initial upward trend of a particular stock before an expected pullback or trend reversal. This reversal is also referred to as the counter-trend. After the trend reversal, you should expect to observe a resumption of the upward trend.

Collect Profits on the Uptrend

It is advisable to wait for the resumption of the uptrend before entering a trade because we have no idea how long a downward trend could last.

Therefore, always watch out for the upward movement, wait for the pullback, and then watch out for the trend to resume and then make a move. This is true and valid for a bullish situation.

To effectively achieve this, you will need to be able to determine the most appropriate entry point. In most cases, this is usually as soon as the upward trend resumes just after the counter-trend. However, you will need to confirm this using risk analysis. The entry point needs to be tested in order to determine the target and assess any possible risks.

You will also need to determine the exit trade point. This is the point at which you will exit the trade should it begin a downward trend. It is also known as the stop-loss point. This approach is necessary if you are to limit your losses. Also, identify the peak or highest point of the new upward trend. This peak should be considered as your take profit point. Once this point is attained, you should take at least some profit because there could be another counter-trend.

If the upward trend continues, then you will need to identify the best possible exit point or profit point so that you ride the momentum even as you lock in some of the profits. This is an excellent approach and is one of the easiest ways of making money as a swing trader. The reward of any trade is equal to the difference between the entry point and the take profit point.

Basically, the potential to earn a profit needs to be about twice the size of any possible losses. If this ratio is lower, then the trade is considered bad, but if it's higher, the ratio is considered great. Therefore, when making a determination on whether a swing trade is worth entering, you should use the risk-reward ratio of 2:1 as the minimum.

The Downtrend

Some traders prefer to enter a bullish market and apply swing trade strategies. Entry into such trade requires the use of a limit order, specifically the buy-stop order. Most traders prefer trading either stocks or options. Call options are preferred in a bearish market as traders do profit under such market conditions. Options trading a bearish market can be rather complicated, but it is an art practiced and favored by many seasoned traders.

Stocks and options on a bearish market tend to follow a zigzag or step-like path. In such a case, a stock will decline in value for a number of days, and then experience resurgence before resuming the downward trend again. With close observation and time, the overall trend can be viewed in much the same way as the upward trend.

Gains Collected on the Downward Trend

First of all, you should only enter a bearish trade after carefully evaluating your risk versus reward ratio. We can compare the entry point in this instance with the stop loss point. If the stock option or stocks attain the lowest price level of the most recent downward trend, then this point will be considered the take profit point, so it is advisable to take profits and exit the trade.

Fading

As a swing trader, you will mostly follow the trend set by a particular stock on the market. Going with the trend is advisable and is what most traders do. You must be super talented or experienced to go against the trend. However, there are traders who do this. Such traders are said to be "fading."

Fading is simply another term for trading against the market trend. There are other terms used to mean the same thing. These include trading the fade, contrarian trading, and counter-trend trading. Sometimes, swing traders choose to trade the fade. This is where they assume a bearish position during an upward trend and a bullish position during a downward trend.

As a trader, you want to exit any fading trades before the end of the counter trends. This is because the trend will resume its normal movement, and your positions could start making losses.

Day Trading Versus Swing Trading

Day trading is similar to swing trading in certain aspects. The major difference between the two is that trades entered in day trading are closed that very same day. Trades usually last only a couple of hours and sometimes even minutes. This is totally different from swing trading where trades can last for days, weeks, and sometimes even longer.

Swing trading requires less time on the trading platforms compared to day trading. You do not need to sit down all day observing your screen and noting all the tiny movements that occur during the day. Day traders can hardly afford to leave the trading platform as they risk losing money.

As a swing trader, you are able to maximize profitability in the short-term by benefiting from most of the market swings. You can also rely solely on technical analysis to carry out trades and still be profitable.

The only major challenge when it comes to day trading is that you can be exposed to unexpected risks on the weekends or overnight. This is likely to happen when major events or announcements are made that can affect stock price movement. You can sometimes lose money on your trades when there is an abrupt or unexpected market reversal. And sometimes you may lose out big time on long-term opportunities by pursuing pretty short-term trends.

In essence, day trading and swing trading are very similar in some aspects. The major difference is the holding time. The minimum holding time with swing trading is overnight while day traders have to close out their trades before the expiry of the trading session. Positions are always limited to a day.

When a position is held overnight, certain things can happen. For instance, the trend could head downwards, or the position could suffer risks like gaps. Both day and swing traders have access to trading margins from their brokers. A margin is simply a loan granted by the broker to clients for purposes of enhancing trades. Swing traders have access to about 50% leverage, which means that a trader can receive a loan of up to 50% from the broker.

Trading Tactics

Swing traders prefer dealing in multiple-day rather than single-day charts. Common chart patterns that are favored by swing traders include triangles, flags, head, and shoulder patterns, cup and handle patterns as well as the moving average crossovers. However, each trader is expected to come up with their own trading strategy that suits their purpose, style, demeanor, and so on.

The best approach is to identify and come up with a strategy that provides one with an edge over numerous other trades. To come up with such a trade, a trader will need to identify suitable trade setups that point towards predictable movements of the chosen asset. Achieving such a feat is never easy, and even the best strategies do fail some of the time.

No trader is victorious on each trade. Even the most successful and well-known traders such as Warren Buffet lose out on some trades. All you need is to identify a suitable and favorable risk versus reward ratio. In fact, to be profitable, you will only require a very favorable risk to reward ratio without the need to be successful in all your trades.

Chapter 2: The Intricacies of Swing Trading

Swing trading has the potential to benefit from explosive price movements of a stock within a pretty limited period of time. Most of the time, a trader will not be concerned about certain things. For instance, you will not need to concern yourself about a company's fundamentals, the kind of services or products they offer, and even their trading name.

As a swing trader, you will be making your trading decisions depending on the demand and supply forces in the marketplace. There are two things that will concern you the most. For starters, is there any money headed towards the chosen stock, or is it hemorrhaging funds? Even as you identify a preferred stock, you will need to find a way to enter a particular trade while not exposing your trading capital to any unhinged risks.

A lot of traders like skipping the basics because they believe they have a good understand and foundation of trading. If you wish to be unsuccessful in your trades, then you can skip this section. Otherwise, all successful traders take the time to learn and refresh their knowledge of swing trading fundamentals.

Swing Trading Tactics

There are certain swing trading tactics that are effective and work well in reality. There are plenty of tactics that work well on paper but do not work reliably in real life. A lot of the time, we will rely on indicators in order to have successful trades. Indicators are among the most useful tools when it comes to swing trading. For instance, the moving average is considered a reliable indicator.

Use of Indicators

There are two indicators considered among the most important in the world of swing trading. These indicators should not be used to inform us of the best trade entry points but simply as guides that point us in the right direction. However, these two are lagging indicators and as such, not the best for our purposes. If you use them for your trades, they will result in inefficient trades that lack precision. However, they remain beneficial and useful most of the time.

There are other indicators available that you can use. These also let you know exact points wherein you should enter the market as well as the best exit points. You get to learn as precisely as possible where to place stop-loss orders and where to locate the profit targets.

A lot of traders have a certain aversion to day trades. They do not have the patience or time that intraday trading requires. Such traders still want to trade stocks and other financial instruments at the market and benefit from short term movements. It is here that swing trading comes in handy.

Swing trading requires you to identify a stock or another financial instrument that has the potential to make you money. Traders do not simply choose stocks to trade at random. They have to know which ones are the most favorable and which ones are not. This requires some skill, so you should learn how to identify the best stocks to invest in.

Trigger Fingers

As a day trader, you need to learn how to react fast just before a stock makes a move. You need to develop trigger fingers so that you can enter a trade at the most appropriate time and without wasting any time. Time wasted could result in a lost opportunity. Basically, the process is about predicting when a stock will move and the moments prior to the movement.

You also need to be aware that swing trading is not about making a home run or simply a long shot. It is more about identifying a trend using certain technical indicators, then using additional indicators to confirm the price movement then eventually identifying entry and exit points. This calls for a better or improved chart reading.

Ways to Identify Stocks for Swing Trading

One of the most crucial things that you need to do in order to be a successful swing trader is to identify ideal stocks or other financial instruments to trade correctly. The first step in identifying ideal stocks is to identify obvious catalysts. A catalyst is an event that can cause a stock price to increase exponentially within a short time period.

Think about events such as economic data points, regulatory announcements, earnings reports, and other scheduled events that can impact the world of finance. Most of these events are predictable and known way ahead of time. Due to this predictability, you are able to know when to keep track of events, get ready, and eventually get into the market. Most swing traders are able to time these events perfectly and proceed to benefit from stock price movements.

In the United States, for instance, traders have already known that on the first Tuesday of each month, the auto industry will release their sales figures. The strength of the sales will help determine whether the stocks will trend upwards or downwards. Major auto companies in the US include Ford Motor Company, General Motors, and Fiat Chrysler among others.

Another thing you have to be on the lookout for is volatility. Volatility is your friend as a swing trader. You should be wary of long upward or downward trends as they provide no clear exit or entry points. However, some volatility will come in handy. When there is some volatility, then you will clearly see the best spots to place stop-loss, profit-take, as well as entry and trade exit points.

Finding Suitable Stocks to Trade

Swing trading can be challenging before you get used to it. Most of the time, you will be working with different tools trying to make the best of prevailing market conditions. One of the benefits of swing trading over day trading is that you will mostly be saving your trading capital through buying and holding for a couple of days.

However, there are some challenges related to holding stocks for days or weeks at a time. One of these challenges includes events and news that occur overnight. However, even with these risks, you are still able to find a suitable stock to trade.

There are three basic approaches used to determine the most appropriate stock depending on your preferred trading style. These are technical analysis, major events or catalysts, and fundamental analysis. You can choose your preferred style to begin your hunt for the ideal stock.

First Step

The first thing you need to do is find out if there are any major events expected to happen. These are events that will have a direct impact on stock prices. For example, earnings reports. It is important to do this because not only are these events predictable but provide an excellent chance for any serious swing trader.

There are a couple of places to check for events. The internet is one such place. Search the internet for upcoming events in the world of finance and sometimes even politics. Political announcements sometimes affect business in a huge way. One of the best websites to check out is www.earningswhispers.com. Others include www.finviz.com, Bloomberg, and CNBC. Most seasoned swing traders also favor the SEC filings websites where they can search for companies that have filed returns.

You will also need to use technical analysis. This is essential if you are to find some potential trades. Technical analysis also comes in handy when there is a known catalyst that can enable a bullish price movement. It provides the necessary information needed to identify suitable trades. It also helps when there is a catalyst that encourages a bullish pattern.

Technical Analysis

This is the best and most popular approach to find trades that are used by most swing traders. Your trading platform should have a screener that you can use. If it does not come with one, then you can use a free one such as Finviz. Start by examining technical patterns on a regular basis and preferably at night in order to note the ones that are just about to break out or rebound.

You can also search for stocks that experienced a large upward movement in price direction followed by a brief pullback. In fact, this is what swing traders do most of the time. They try to identify a stock that has had a major rally followed by a pullback.

Spend some time filtering through different stocks and identify a couple that you can swing trade. Once this is done, you will then have to come up with a trading plan. A good trading plan implies that you have determined an appropriate entry point, the most suitable stop-loss point, and the best point to collect profits. It is crucial to consolidate your gains at some point even if the stock continues to increase its price. Should this be the case, then you should consolidate your profits then get back in with a new plan.

Having a good trading plan is crucial for your success. Trading without one is akin to setting yourself up for failure. Therefore, come up with a plan and a reliable risk management strategy. Risk management helps you manage the exposure of your trading capital so that you limit your losses. Without proper risk management, you could lose most of your trading capital and put a strain on your trading.

Executing a Trade

Now that you have identified a stock to trade and come up with a trading plan, the next step should be to execute the trade. As soon as you do, you will have to keep yourself updated with the latest happening in the worlds of finance and perhaps even politics. Watch out for any upcoming events and then weight their strengths in terms of affecting your stock's price movement.

Also, be on the lookout for volatility as this is your friend. A prolonged uptrend is never a good thing. When a stock has an uptrend, you should hope to see a reversal in direction for a brief period of time before the uptrend resumes. This counter trend provides excellent entry points. It also provides information on potential profit-take points to exit trades or stop-loss points.

You will eventually have to exit your trades. Hopefully, these will have earned you some attractive profits in a short period of time. After exiting your trades, you need to take a pen and a notebook and then note down all the things that took place. Write down what steps you took, what worked for you, and possibly what did not work. Put down the reasons that affected your trades and if they were profitable or not.

If you do not write down details of the trade explaining what worked and what didn't, then you are very likely to repeat any mistakes in your next trade. Any lesson learned has to be entered into a journal. This way, you will note all the positives as well as any negatives so as to improve future trades.

The best aspect of swing trading is that you require less energy and less time to trade compared to day trading. It strikes a nice balance between long term trading and day trading. If you are concerned about holding overnight positions, then you need to know that swing trading is one of the most popular and most profitable forms of generating income and profitability.

Swing Trading Versus High-Frequency Trading

As a trader, you need to learn more about high-frequency trading or HFT. Once you learn more about swing trading and are able to predict movements accurately and take profits, you can improve your performance via HFT. Basically, high-frequency trading refers to a platform that programs the trading process.

The platform makes use of powerful computers that execute trades on behalf of a trader. As a swing trader, you may want to be profitable in a fast and stress-free manner. The best approach is to let this system of powerful computers with programmed software to execute trades on your behalf.

HFT transacts numerous trades and executes orders in only a few seconds. The computers are powered by powerful software programs that run complex algorithms. These algorithms mostly analyze the markets then execute trades depending on the conditions in the market. Ordinarily, the trader who executes trades the fastest ends up earning more compared to slower counterparts.

Back in the day, stock markets and exchanges started to invite companies to add liquidity to the market. To do this effectively, they started to offer incentives to willing companies. In fact, some exchanges had designated liquidity providers whose main purpose was to ensure a liquid market. This is one where traders can enter, conduct their business and exit without any concerns.

Companies providing liquidity were paid some money by the exchanges. Since there are numerous transactions that take place on a daily basis, the liquidity providers, who are paid per transaction, earn large sums of money. Today, most stock exchanges are pretty liquid. Liquidity is often introduced by large investment companies, especially fund management companies.

Advantages of Using High-Frequency Trading

There are numerous benefits of HFT. One of these is that it has resulted in very liquid markets. Markets need to be liquid if traders are to come and trade. A liquid market means they can convert their shares, stocks, and profits into immediate cash and back to stocks.

It has resulted in the removal of the bid-ask spreads, which previously were rather small. The stock markets introduced a small operating fee for HFT users, and this saw the spreads increase in size.

However, there are those who are unhappy with HFT trades. For instance, HFT has rendered a lot of dealers and brokers jobless. They have instead been replaced by machines that execute trades on their behalf. Machines now make numerous trade decisions that were previously made by traders or brokers. In some cases, HFT has resulted in major losses such as the market crash of May 2010. Back then, the DJIA or Dow Jones Industrial Average suffered massive losses all which were eventually attributed to a massive order. This order, according to a government-sanctioned investigation, was shown to have been as a result of the crash. This is why there are some people who still have misgivings about it.

Drawbacks of Using High-Frequency Trading

There have been some issues surrounding HFT or high-frequency trading. There has been a lot of criticism directed at this trading system. Many experts concede that it has taken away jobs that were ordinarily the reserve of dealers and brokers.

Most decisions are made via algorithms and mathematical models designed and managed through software programs. These take away the aspects of human interactions and decisions. Also, all decisions occur within milliseconds, which can have a great impact on the market for no real reason. There is a good real-life example of this.

Back in 2010, DJIA or Dow Jones Industrial Average had its worst loss in a single trading day. On May 6th of the same year, it lost over 1000 points within a period of 20 minutes before it picked momentum once again. An investigation by the regulator revealed that a client had placed a massive automated order using the HFT system which saw the loss incurred by DJIA.

Also, some experts opine that High-Frequency Trading provides opportunities to big companies and large conglomerates to benefit and profit at the expense of small, medium size, and institution retail traders. This means that ordinary traders like you and

I are unable to profit from the markets like we should because opportunities are taken up by these large investors.

There is also concern and doubt regarding the liquidity introduced to the markets by HFT. Many people term it "ghost liquidity" because the liquidity is available one moment and then the next moment it is all gone. This means traders across the markets are unable to access the liquidity.

In brief, we can conclude that high-frequency trading is simply a software program designed to execute a large number of trades in a short period of time. This program actually introduces new liquidity into the markets and gets rid of the minute bid-ask spreads. The main challenges that this platform introduces are criticisms regarding non-existent liquidity and favoring large, institutional investors over retail investors.

Swing Trading Versus Position Trading

Position trading refers to the trading style where a trader holds a position in the markets for a long time. This time period ranges from a number of weeks to months and sometimes even years. This makes a clear difference between day traders, swing traders, and position traders.

Position traders do not care much about fluctuations in the short term. They are also not concerned about the fundamentals of a company or the happenings of the day. News of an economic or political nature is of least concern because their long term positions are not likely to be affected.

Position traders also do not engage in regular and active trading like other traders. They place a few trades, forget about them, and go about their businesses. In fact, they only trade a couple of times a year. This type of trading brings them close to long-term, buy-and-hold investors. Their main concerns are events that can have a direct impact on their positions.

This trading method offers traders an excellent opportunity to invest in stocks and other financial assets in the long term. However, it is necessary to note that long-term positions do face potential risks even though they stand excellent chances of profit.

Most traders enter this type of trade for investment rather than trade purposes. Many position traders prefer long-term trades over speculation. They put their money in share portfolios a lot of the time. However, their investment opportunities are limited when they choose CDs as these have certain time limitations.

Technical and Fundamental Analysis

Most of the time, position traders use technical analysis, together with fundamental analysis, to research and explore potential trends in the market as well as any associated risks prior to assuming a position. They analyze price charts using a number of strategies in order to come up with credible predictions regarding market conditions.

1. Support and Resistance

One of the more popular trading strategies used by position traders is support and resistance. This strategy enables position traders to learn about when a stock's price is likely to enter into either an upward or downward trend. Position traders will assess the outcome of the strategy to determine whether to open a position on a particular stock or other assets. They also use the same assessment to determine when to exit a position.

Some common terms that position traders use and rely on include resistance level and support level. Support level refers to the price that a stock or other asset never drops below since most buyers tend to purchase at this price. The same is true with the resistance level. This is exactly where the price or value of an asset stops to rise. Using this information, traders can determine when to take profit and close their positions. This is instead of maintaining current positions at the risk of a price decrease.

Traders use this strategy of support and resistance to analyze and examine chart patterns. If you are an aspiring trader, then this is a technique that you should learn. It will come in handy and will enable you to make the important decisions that are crucial to your trades. If you wish to try out the support and resistance strategy, then you have to consider a couple of factors.

a) The most trusted source for pointing out support and resistance levels is the historical price. The usual practice is to use periods of substantial reductions and gains in the stock price as reliable pointers of future price movement.

b) Also, past support and resistance levels can be used by position traders to determine future price movement. For instance, when a support level is overcome, it could easily become a resistance level in the future.

c) In addition, we could also count on other technical indicators to provide unprecedented resistance and supply levels that can alter a stock's price. A good example is the Fibonacci retracements.

2. Breakout Strategy

Apart from the support and resistance levels strategy, position traders can also rely on the breakout strategy. This is a strategy where a trader does endeavor to enter a position in the initial stages of a trend. This particular strategy is popularly used to provide the foundation needed by traders when it comes to large price movements.

As a breakout position trader, you will start by taking a long position on a stock once it breaks beyond the prevailing resistance levels. Alternatively, you will assume a short position once the price of the stock drops to levels below that of support. If you wish to be successful using this approach, then you will have to be pretty sharp at noting periods when there are market support and resistance.

3. Range Trading Strategy

This is yet another excellent strategy used by position traders. It is best applied in markets that are regularly moving up and down. Traders who benefit the most from this specific strategy are Forex traders because Forex markets often lack an obvious and clear trend.

This strategy is best for traders who have identified assets or stocks that have nee oversold and overbought. The purpose here is to dispose of the over-purchased assets and purchased oversold stocks. We can define an overbought asset as that whose price is very close to resistance levels while an oversold one is that which is close to support levels.

4. Pullback and Retracement Strategy

A pullback can be defined as a short-term, non-permanent reversal or dip in a stock's mostly upward movement. Traders can apply this strategy when they wish to capitalize on such pauses or fallbacks in a largely upward trend of a stock's price. The purpose here is to purchase stocks or other instruments at low prices then sell at much higher prices once the price resumes its upward movement.

Traders sometimes refer to pullbacks as retracements. However, these should never be mistaken for reversals. A reversal is more of a longer-term or sometimes even permanent deviation away from the prevailing price movement. Fibonacci retracement can be used to determine if a reversal in a prevailing market trend is an actual reversal or permanent deviation.

Fibonacci Retracement Application for Position Traders

The term Fibonacci retracement refers to a type of technical analysis that is useful to position traders and all other traders. Fibonacci retracement enables position traders to determine the best time to enter and exit a position. Identifying the Fibonacci retracements requires a series of lines to be drawn on a stock's price chart. These lines will then be used to identify levels of resistance and support. These are the points that will be used by traders to determine where to enter and exit positions.

Summary

In summary, we can state that position trading includes undertaking serious technical and fundamental analysis. It also requires a deep understanding of the financial markets. We observe the importance of support and resistance levels. These are useful indicators and inform traders about the most appropriate points when the price movement of a stock is likely to dip or trend downwards. There are a couple of strategies that are perfect for position trading. These are range trading, breakout trading, and pullback trading strategies.

Investment and Margin Accounts

Traders need to open an account with a broker before they can begin trading. As an aspiring trader, you need to learn how to identify brokers and choosing the best account for trading purposes. One of the accounts that you can have is a margin account.

A margin account can be defined as a brokerage account where the broker lends you funds which you will use for trading purposes. The funds are made available to you as a trader so that you can place more trades and be more profitable. The money is considered to be a loan whose collateral includes any cash in your account as well as other stocks and securities that you have in your account.

There is an interest often charged on loan. This interest is usually paid off periodically together with the principal amount. Since you are trading the markets using borrowed money, you can expect to make a lot more profits especially if your strategy is profitable and has proven successful in the past. Such a loan is also considered leverage which plenty of traders hope for. If you have $10,000 in your trading account and hoping to make a profit of $2,000, then think what difference an additional $30,000 will do to your bottom line.

Details of Margin Accounts

Investors will use leverage funds to invest in additional securities such as stocks. With time, those securities are bound to earn a profit. They will appreciate in value over time and earn you a decent income. This income will be much larger because of leverage. This is the reason why traders prefer margin accounts. It gives them an undue advantage over other traders.

Therefore, obtaining a margin account is equivalent to getting a loan from your broker with the aim of purchasing stocks. Such an account is completely different from a normal account where you only trade using your own funds. Now if the profit generated by a trading account is in excess of interest charged on the borrowed funds, then the advantage of the account is evident.

However, if the leverage does not result in profitability and the trader is unable to repay the borrowed funds plus interest, then the loan will become outstanding. This will have negative consequences on your account. For instance, if the securities purchased lose value or basically a trade is not profitable, then the trader will be said to be underwater and will have to find ways of repaying the borrowed funds.

In the unfortunate event that the equity levels of the margin account fall below what the broker considered maintenance margin, then the trader or client will very likely receive a margin call from the brokerage firm. This usually happens after a couple of days, such as three or less. An investor will be required to provide more funds in their account or possibly liquidate some of their financial assets like stocks in order to recover the lost funds.

As per the law, you are required to sign some documents provided by the broker before opening a margin account. Often times brokerage firms provide forms which you are required to fill out when signing up for an account. However, in most cases, there is a separate form for those opening a margin account. There are also additional requirements such as a first-time deposit of about $2,000. Some brokerage firms demand more than this amount.

It is after the account is open that you are allowed to borrow close to 50% of your deposit. However, you do not necessarily have to borrow the entire 50% available to you. Many traders opt for amounts between 10% and 25%. Traders are allowed to keep the borrowed funds for any period of time just long as they keep the terms of the agreement. Basically, when you make a profit from the sale of stocks and so on, the funds will first be used to clear your debt in incremental amounts until the entire amount is paid.

Caution: As an investor with a margin account, you are more likely to lose money than be profitable. As such, you should only own such an account if you are a seasoned trader with years of verifiable profitability. Traders who open margin accounts are often sophisticated investors who possess a deeper understanding of the markets as well as the risks inherent and requirements of a margin account.

Maintenance Margin

The term maintenance margin refers to a minimum amount that must be maintained in a margin account at all times. Also, all margin securities in a margin account are all taken as collateral. However, whenever you make profits through trading activity via the account, some of the profit is used to offset the loan. Eventually, the debt amount will be paid in full, and your trading capital will increase significantly.

Margin amounts should be used to invest or trade in short-term opportunities with huge potential returns. Try and avoid long-term investment using margin because the chances of profitability do decrease with each passing day. Also, it is not all securities that can be purchased using margin funds. Regulations approved by the government regulator have clearly indicated which stocks can be bought and which ones are out of bounds.

For instance, penny stocks cannot be purchased using margin funds. Other forbidden stocks include IPOs or initial public offerings and over the counter BB securities. The reason is that all these securities are exposed to high everyday risks. Brokers sometimes add their own stocks to the list. They can decide which stocks you may not trade or invest in using margin funds. Therefore, always check and confirm which securities qualify before trading. Also, the minimum balance required of $2,000 must be maintained at all costs.

Additional Financial Products

You are allowed to purchase or invest and trade in other products apart from stocks. These include futures, currencies, options, and so on. When it comes to these other securities, there may be additional requirements on your account balance. Some brokers may want additional deposits if they are concerned about certain risky investments like futures, for instance. Therefore, always check with your broker before buying.

Investing Versus Trading

Trading and investing have numerous similarities. In both instances, an individual or institution uses financial resources to make a profit. However, a closer look at the two shows they are very different from each other. While both a trader and an investor do seek to make a profit from investing in the markets, investors often choose to make huge returns over a prolonged period of time, while traders take smaller and frequent profits over a short period of time.

Investment Accounts

The main aim of an investment account is to generate profits and gradually build wealth over time. This is often achieved through the purchase of stocks and other financial assets over a period of time. Every investor looks to generate wealth for the long term.

Investors often have different reasons for generating funds. Some wish to start businesses others want to invest in real estate, and so on. One of the best ways of saving and generating funds in the long term is to reinvest interest and also compound the investments. Investors also diversify their portfolios into plenty of other products including stocks, bonds, options, mutual funds, indexes, and so on.

Investment accounts hold assets and funds for lengthy periods of time. It can take years and sometimes decades before profits are accessed. Investors take advantage of opportunities, including stock splits, dividends, and interests that accrue over time. Of course, markets do fluctuate from time to time. However, investment accounts are able to override these challenges to grow exponentially over time. Moreover, the compounding of investments ensures that such challenges are overcome. Examples of investment accounts include IRA accounts and 401(K) accounts.

Trading Accounts

Trading accounts include most of all the other accounts discussed previously. These accounts include a lot of small but regular and frequent transactions. The main aim of these accounts is to generate returns that are higher than the long-term or buy-and-hold accounts.

Investors can be happy receiving 10% to 15% return annually, but traders prefer about 10% return each month. Profits on trading accounts normally accrue from buying small amounts at low prices and then selling the same at higher prices. These trades are often carried out in the shortest periods of time.

Trading styles basically refer to the holding time or amount of time between the purchase and sale of securities. Trade accounts, therefore, include day traders, swing traders, position traders, and scalp traders. Scalp traders hold positions in the markets for only a couple of seconds or minutes. There are certain factors that determine the choice of trading style. These include personality, trading experience, and levels of risk tolerance.

Buy Long or Sell Short

As a trader, you need to learn more about long and short buying and selling. Trades usually commence via purchase first or selling first. To define the terms appropriately, we need to learn about the meaning and implication of each.

Long position: When you assume a long position on a stock, the implication here is that you own the security and it belongs to you. There is no debt on it. Therefore, when a trader buys an asset, he has taken a long position on the asset. In this instance, he hopes that the asset price will appreciate so that he can sell it at a higher price.

Short position: We also have a short position where a trader actually sells stocks that he or she does not own. These are stocks or financial instruments that belong to another. Selling short simply means selling in the hope of making money from the sale in order to repay the owner and make a profit in the process.

Short sales occur when a trader is trading the markets, sees an opportunity but lacks the funds or means to execute the trade. Many experienced traders come across opportunities they believe are profitable. In such instances, they get into an agreement with their broker to access stocks they do not own.

Day traders are often associated with short sales. They often sell stocks then purchase them hoping to benefit from the price difference. They sell stocks that they do not own at a high price and then buy back the same stocks when the price falls. While this can be profitable, it is a risky venture that should only be practiced by seasoned traders.

Short sales by traders are often settled by delivery of the "borrowed" security back to the real owner. Most stocks that are sold short often belong to investors but are held by brokers. As a trader, if you wish to short sell, then you first need to identify an opportunity in the market. You will then need to access the stock so that you can sell it without owning it. This is of course after your market analysis shows some profit potential.

Others who also engage in short selling are market makers. Market makers are also known as liquidity providers. They do this in order to mitigate the risk of a long position on the same stock or in response to unexpected demand. Market makers hope to benefit financially from a bid-offer spread.

Traders who engage in short selling can borrow stocks from brokerage firms. Brokerage firms often have an inventory of stocks lying around. Some of these belong to the brokerage while others belong to other long-term investors. It is important to note that even as you gain access to stocks that you do now own, there are certain rules and conditions attached. These include fees and other charges as well as rules. For instance, you can expect to be charged a certain fee for the privilege. You will also be required to pay any dividend due to the stock's owner while the stocks are under your control.

Chapter 3: Swing Trading Systems and Tools

Huge profits are made when there are large swings in the market. This is according to Jesse Livermore, who is among the most successful traders of all time. He chose to use swing trading strategies that work extremely well and in the process made huge returns. He was able to achieve amazing results in the course of his trading career and made a fortune in the process.

A lot of traders are always searching for the best trading systems and ways they can develop these systems to suit their trading styles. Fortunately, there is a process that any trader can use in order to discover their preferred trading mode and system.

Novice traders are often excited at the prospect of swing trading. They are usually extremely eager to get started thinking about all the money out there waiting to be made. People are generally attracted to the markets because of the opportunity to make money on a regular basis.

Perseverance

At the onset, most traders believe that trading is easy and straightforward. Many get into the markets after reading a blog or book and getting inspired by the words they read. Often there is a story about a successful individual who managed to hack the markets and earn a fortune. However, with time, some realize that things are not that easy or straightforward. Some will quit, and only the most determined will remain.

Trading requires hard work and dedication. It also requires patience as well as experimenting with different styles until a trader identifies one that suits him the most. Take some time and do your research. Learn as much as you can about the markets. However, do not start searching for the easiest way out because nothing in life is easy.

Other important factors that affect the choice of a trading system include money management, risk control, and positive expectancy. When a trader is well aware of these crucial trading aspects, they begin to think about incorporating them into a strategy and trading system. With a good system and plan, a trader is able to fit in a trading plan that works for him or her in the long term. Get-rich-quick thoughts disappear pretty fast as reality hits home.

Identifying Best Strategies for Profitability

There are plenty of small but crucial things you can do as a swing trader to improve your success. For instance, you could begin by identifying the location of the swing low and swing high positions on a particular chart. If you are able to note the swings accurately, then you will be able to place accurate trades, which will increase your profitability greatly.

Swing Highs and Swing Lows

Swing highs and swing lows are also referred to as SHSL. This refers to the price action where multiple bars and candlesticks are joined together so that they are viewed as a single move in a given direction. The movement is generally known as a leg. Sometimes, it is also known as swing or a move. This is where the term swing originates from.

The swing represents a single part of the price action in a particular direction. This swing is always closely countered by a swing in the opposite direction. Sometimes, this movement is sideways rather than back and forth. As it is, price moves back and forth in the market. In other words, it swings back and forth and hence, the term swing. The highest point of a swing is the swing high while the lowest point is known as the swing low.

How to Identify Swings

The market is constantly in motion. A swing occurs when there are two consecutive lower highs and lower lows or when there are two consecutive higher lows and higher highs. Remember that swings appear in all manner of shapes and sizes. However, the rule on how to identify them is very simple. Simply look for consecutive higher highs and higher lows or consecutive lower highs and lower lows.

Swings are bullish if the general movement is upwards and bearish if the general movement is downwards. Sometimes, a new low will appear when the trend is upwards. At other times a new high will appear when the general trend is headed downwards. When this happens, you should not be worried or concerned as these are considered false swings. Unless there are consecutive highs or lows, then ignore everything else.

Using Swings to Increase Profitability

We have learned how to identify swings in the market. Now we need to apply this knowledge in order to be profitable. The first step is to place your stop loss points. This should be slightly above the higher high for a bearish situation and below the lowest low in a bullish situation.

Also, the correct and accurate swing highs and swing lows provide an opportunity to draw Fibonacci extensions. These lines will enable you to identify target areas of high probability. As such, it becomes possible to place our take profit and stop loss points on our charts. Remember Livermore? The gentleman said to be one of the most successful traders ever? Back in 19 29, he managed to make about $100 million. In today's terms, this is equivalent to almost $1.4 billion. That is a lot of money, even for an experienced trader.

If you learn about the best trading systems, then you too can make plenty of money in today's prevailing marketing rates. You could always trade with the market trend or against it. Remember that it is always advisable to follow the trend rather than the opposite. Only oppose the trend if you are an experienced swing trader and know what you are doing exactly. Key will be identifying the best entry points into a trade and the best places to collect profits as well as exit trades.

Before you begin your swing trading ventures, ensure that you come up with a tested plan that you can implement. Therefore, test your preferred systems and strategies and ensure that they are working as desired. This way, you will be able to prepare appropriately and trade successfully and profitably over time.

Swing traders are always searching for conditions in the markets where stock prices are looking to swing either downwards or possibly upwards. There are numerous technical indicators that are available to enhance your trades. Indicators used in swing trading are basically essential in identifying trends in the market between certain trading periods.

These trading periods that range anywhere from 3 to 15 are then analyzed using our technical indicators in order to determine the presence or otherwise of resistance and support levels. If these have actually materialized and are clearly visible, then we can proceed to make other determinations.

At this stage, you will also need to determine whether any trend is bullish or bearish. You will also need to be on the lookout for a reversal because without one, you will not be able to enter a trade. Reversals are also referred to as countertrends or pullbacks. As soon as we can clearly point out the reversal, then we can easily identify the appropriate entry point.

The entry point should be the point where the pullback is just about to come to an end, and the trend is about to pick up again. Being able to determine these points is really crucial. This same approach is the very same one used by Jesse Livermore to earn his wealth.

Benefits

Swing trading offers some of the best risks to reward opportunities compared to other trading strategies. This means that for a smaller amount, you will stand to win a much larger profit. Trading is a risky venture, but swing trading has a better payoff compared to others. As such, you stand to make more money at reduced risks compared to traders using different trading styles like day traders or position traders.

Another benefit is that a lot of intraday noise will be eliminated using this approach. Smart money traders are always on the lookout for big swings, and this is what you will also be doing. This approach is less stressful and potentially more profitable compared to other strategies.

You will also have a lot of time in your hands compared to other traders. Day traders and others often spend hours each day glued to their screens. Their days are not just spent staring at the screen, but their stress levels are extremely high. Constant stress will result in fast burn-out and emotional trading, which are not good for successful long-term trading.

Best Indicators for Swing Traders

There are plenty of indicators that traders and investors use to enhance their trades. We shall review just a few of these and discover the best way of applying them to our trades in order to maximize profitability. It is crucial to understand that none of these indicators will make you profitable from the onset. Therefore, do not stress over trying to find the best or most profitable trade indicators. Instead, focus more on learning about a couple of extremely effective indicators as well as the strategies and methods used alongside them. Experts believe that trading strategies are more profitable when you apply the few indicators that you have mastered.

1. Moving Averages

Moving averages are among the most important trade indicators used by swing traders. They are defined as lines drawn across a chart and are determined based on previous prices. Moving averages are really to understand, yet they are absolutely useful when it comes to trading the markets. They are extremely useful to all kinds of traders, including swing traders, day traders, intra-day traders, and long-term investors.

You need to ensure that you have a number of moving averages plotted across your trading charts all with different time periods. For instance, you can have the 100-day moving average, the 50-day, and the 9-day MA. This way, you will obtain a much broader overview of the market and be able to identify much stronger reversals and trends.

Once you have plotted and drawn the moving averages on your charts, you can then use them for a number of purposes. The first is to identify the strength of a trend. Basically, what you need to do is to observe the lines and gauge their distance from the current stock price.

A trend is considered weak if the trend and the current price are far from the relative MA. The farther they are then, the weaker the trend is. This makes it easier for traders to note any possible reversals and also identify exit and entry points. You should use Moving Averages together with additional indicators—for instance, the volume.

Moving averages can also be used to identify trend reversals. When you plot multiple moving averages, they are bound to cross. If they do, then this implies a couple of things. For instance, crossing MA lines indicate a trend reversal. If these cross after an uptrend, then it means that the trend is about to change direction and a bearish one is about to appear.

However, some trend reversals are never real, so you have to be careful before calling out one. Many traders are often caught off guard by these false reversals. Therefore, confirm them before trading using other tools and methods. Even then, the moving average is a very vital indicator. They enable traders to get a true feel and understanding of the markets.

2. RSI – Relative Strength Index

Another crucial indicator that is commonly used by swing traders and other traders is the RSI or relative strength index. This index is also an indicator that evaluates the strength of the price of a security that you may be interested in. The figure indicated is relative and provides traders with a picture of how the stock is performing relative to the markets. You will need information regarding volatility and past performance. All traders, regardless of their trading styles, need this useful indicator. Using this relative evaluation tool gives you a figure that lies between 1 and 100.

Tips on RSI Use

The relative strength index is ideally used for identifying divergence. Divergence is used by traders to note trend reversals. We can say that divergence is a disagreement or difference between two points. There are bearish and bullish divergent signals. Very large and fast movements in the markets sometimes produce false signals. This is why it advisable to always use indicators together with other tools.

You can also use the RSI to identify oversold and overbought conditions. It is crucial that you are able to identify these conditions as you trade because you will easily identify corrections and reversals. Sometimes, securities are overbought at the markets—when this situation occurs, it means that there is a possible trend reversal, and usually the emerging trend is bearish. This is often a market correction. Basically, when a security is oversold, it signals a correction or bullish trend reversal. However, when it's overbought, it introduces a bearish trend reversal.

The theory aspect of this condition requires a ratio of 70:30. This translates to 70% overvalued or over purchased and 30% undervalued or oversold. However, in some cases, you might be safer going with a ratio of 80:20 just to prevent false breakouts.

3. Volume

When trading, the volume is a crucial indicator and constitutes a major part of any trading strategy. As a trader, you want to always target stocks with high volumes as these are considered liquid. How many traders, especially new ones, often disregard volume and look at other indicators instead.

While volume is great for liquidity purposes, it is also desirable for trend. A good trend should be supported by volume. A large part of any stock's volume should constitute part of any trend for it to be a true and reliable trend.

Most of the time traders will observe a trend based on price action. You need to also be on the lookout for new money which means additional players and volume. If you note significant volumes contributing to a trend, then you can be confident about your analysis. Even when it comes to a downtrend, there should be sufficient volumes visible for it to be considered trustworthy. A lack of volume simply means a stock has either been undervalued or overvalued.

4. Bollinger Bands Indicator

One of the most important indicators that you will need is the Bollinger band indicator. It is a technical indicator that performs two crucial purposes. The first is to identify sections of the market that are overbought and oversold. The other purpose is to check the market's volatility.

This indicator consists of 3 distinct moving averages. There is a central one which is an SMA or simple moving average and then there two on each side of the SMA. These are also moving averages but are plotted on either side of the central SMA about 2 standard deviations away. These bands can be clearly viewed in the diagram below.

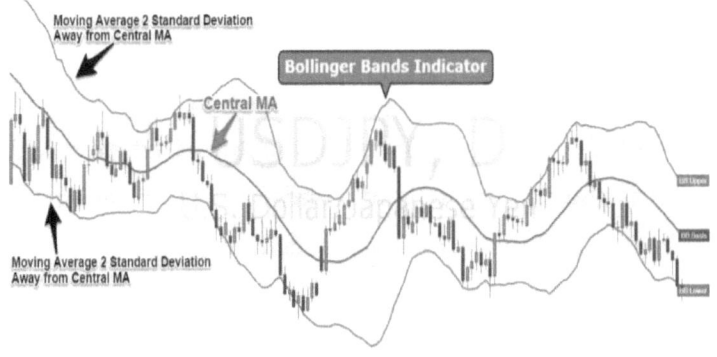

5. Accumulation and Distribution Line

Another indicator that is widely used by swing traders is the accumulation/distribution line. This indicator is generally used to track the money flow within a security. The money that flows into and out of a particular stock provides useful information for your analysis.

The accumulation/distribution indicator compares very well with another indicator, the OBV, or the on-balance volume indicator. The difference, in this case, is that it considers the trading range as well as the closing price of a stock. The OBV only considers the trading range for a given period.

When a security closes out close to its high, then the accumulation/distribution indicator will add weight to the stock value compared to closing out close to the mid-point. Depending on your needs and sometimes the calculations, you may also want to use the OBV indicator.

You can use this indicator to confirm an upward trend. For instance, when it is trending upwards, you will observe buying interest because the security will close at a point that is higher than the mid-range. However, when it closes at a point that is lower than the mid-range, then the volume is indicated as negative, and this indicates a declining trend.

While using this indicator, you will also want to be on the lookout for divergence. When the accumulation/distribution begins to decline while the price is going up, then you should be careful because this signals a possible reversal. On the other hand, if the trend starts to ascend while the price is falling, then this probably indicates a possible price rise in the near future. It is advisable to ensure that your internet and other connections are extremely fast, especially when using these indicators, as time is essential.

6. The Average Directional Index, ADX

Another tool or indicator that is widely used by swing traders is the average directional index, the ADX. This indicator is basically a trend indicator, and its purpose is largely to check the momentum and strength of a trend. A trend is believed to have directional strength if the ADX value is equal to or higher than 40. The directional could be upwards or downward based on the general price direction. However, when the ADX value is below 20, then we can say that there is no trend or there is one, but it is weak and unreliable.

You will notice the ADX line on your charts as it is the main line and is often black in color. There are other lines that can be shown additionally. These lines are DI- and DI+ and in most cases are green and red in color, respectively. You can use all the three lines to track both the momentum and the trend direction.

7. Aroon Technical Indicator

Another useful indicator that you can use is the Aroon indicator. This is a technical indicator designed to check if a particular financial security is trending. It also checks to find out whether the security's price is achieving new lows or new highs over a given period of time.

You can also use this technical indicator to discover the onset of a new trend. It features two distinct lines, which are the "Aroon down" line and the "Aroon up" line. A trend is noted when the "Aroon up" line traverses across the "Aroon down" line. To confirm the trend, then the "Aroon up" line will get to 100-point mark and stay there.

The reverse holds water as well. When the "Aroon down" line cuts below the "Aroon up" line, then we can presume a downward trend. To confirm this, we should note the line that is getting close to the 100-point mark and staying there.

This popular trading tool comes with a calculator which you can use to determine a few things. If the trend is bullish or bearish, then the calculator will let you know. The formulas used to determine this refer to the most recent highs and lows. When the Aroon values are high, then recent values were used; when they are low, the values used were less recent. Typical Aroon values vary between 0 and 100. Figures that are close to 0 indicate a weak trend while those closer to 100 indicate a strong trend.

The bullish and bearish Aroon indicators can be converted into one oscillator. This is done by making the bearish one range from 0 to -100 while the bullish one ranges from 100 to 0. The combined indicator will then oscillate between 100 and -100. 100 will indicate a strong trend, 0 means there is no trend while -100 implies a negative or downward trend.

This trading tool is pretty easy to use. What you need to is first obtain the necessary figures then plot these on the relevant chart. When you then plot these figures on the chart, watch out for the two key levels. These are 30 and 70. Anything above the 70-point mark means the trend is solid while anything below 30 implies a weak trend.

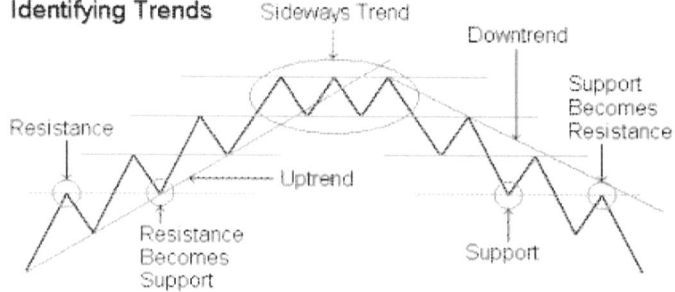

Identifying Trends Sideways Trend Downtrend

Resistance Uptrend Support Becomes Resistance

Resistance Becomes Support Support

Trading Platforms

Trading platforms are the actual platforms or software programs that enable traders to place their trades and monitor their accounts. An electronic trading platform is a computer program or a website with a user interface where traders place financial trades.

As a swing trader, you will use this platform to enter, close, exit, and manage your positions. This is often done via an intermediary such as your broker. Most traders use online platforms which are overseen and offered by brokerage firms. Brokers charge a fee when you use their platforms, but sometimes they offer discounts to traders who make a certain number of trades each month or those with funded accounts.

Basic Swing Trading Platforms

Trading platforms provide traders with the opportunity to place trades and monitor their accounts. There is a variety of platforms available to swing traders. They come with a number of different features. These include premium research functions, a news feed, charting tools, and even real-time price quotes. These additional features and tools enhance a trader's performance and make it easier to execute trades faster and accurately. Most platforms available today are designed for different financial instruments like Forex, stocks, futures, and options.

We basically have two different types of platforms. These are commercial platforms and prop platforms. Commercial platforms are mostly used by traders such as swing traders, retail investors, and day traders. They are largely easy to use and come with a myriad of features such as charts and a news feed.

We also have prop platforms. These are platforms that are customized for specific users, such as institutional investors and large brokerage firms. Apparently, their needs are much different compared to those of small traders and retail investors. The prop platforms are designed to take into consideration the different needs of these special clients.

As a swing trader, you will most likely use commercial platforms provided by different brokerage firms. Even then, there are some things that you need to be on the lookout before choosing one. For instance, what are the included features? How about costs and fees charged? Also, different traders will require different tools on their platforms. There are certain tools that are suitable for day and swing traders, while others are more suitable for options and futures traders.

When selecting a platform, always watch out for the fees charged. As a small-scale, retail swing trader, you want to trade on one that charges low and affordable fees. However, sometimes there are certain trade-offs. For instance, some platforms charge low fees, but they lack certain crucial features or provide poor services. Others may seem expensive but provide crucial features, including research tools and excellent services. Hence, you will need to consider all these factors before eventually selecting a suitable trading platform.

There is yet another crucial point to keep in mind when selecting a trading platform. Some platforms are available only through specific brokers or intermediaries. Other platforms are universal and work with different brokerage platforms and intermediaries across the board. Traders also select trading platforms based on their own personal styles and preferences.

You should find out if there are any particular requirements or conditions that require to be fulfilled. For instance, some platforms require traders to maintain at least $25, 000 in their trading accounts in the form of equity and possibly cash as well. In this instance, a trader may then receive approval for credit which is also known as margin.

Examples of Swing Trading Platforms

1. The Home Trading System

The home trading system is an algorithm and trading software designed to improve performance. Using this system, you can expect to make smarter, faster, and better trading decisions. This particular platform comes with innovative features and a custom algorithm that combines seamlessly to provide a real-time, fully integrated trading platform. You are bound to benefit from this platform and experience the benefits of seamless trading complete with all the features that you need.

The platform is completely compatible with some of the most dynamic and highly reliable charting tool. It is able to work with all kinds of markets from stocks to Forex and indices. The platform is compatible with a variety of bars such as range and momentum bars as well as tick charts.

The designers of this platform took great care to consider all the different kinds of traders. This is why this specific platform is suitable for day traders, swing traders, Forex traders, retail investors, and long-term traders. The Home Trading System constitutes a modular platform that consists of different core features. A lot of these features can easily be switched off and on depending on the situation or to suit a particular requirement.

One of the advantages of this platform is that it endeavors to make trading extremely simply. For instance, the algorithm automatically colors the candlesticks or bars a red or blue color in order to provide a clear view of the market conditions and trends. The system will continue following the trends and mark any major changes in a contrasting color. For instance, whenever there is a trigger bar, these will appear in a different color so that it is clear to you the trader that there is definite variation in the trend.

This color feature not only makes trading easy but also improves your trading psychology so that you can trade with very little worry. Other desirable parameters that are essential to your trades are also provided on the platform. For instance, you need accurate and reliable trading signals delivered at the right time. Fortunately, the Home Trading System is designed to provide these signals in a timely and accurate manner.

When there is a turning point in the momentum of a particular stock in the markets, then this will be detected, and a change of color will clearly indicate the turning point. You will be able to see a blue color with contrasting orange color pointing out areas of interest. The dots will indicate the entry points, exit points, collect profit points and so on. A stopping point is also indicated just in case the trade does not work out as planned and you need to exit.

2. The Entry Zone Platform

We also have a swing trading platform known as the Entry Zone. This platform has been around for a while but has recently undergone a complete overhaul. It has received a new design to address the needs of swing traders specifically. There is no trader in the entire world who wants to join an over-extended market even when it features a large stop-loss point.

One of the main benefits of this specific platform is that it helps eliminate the challenge of entering an overly extended market. It starts by first checking for a pullback. It does this by accessing the 60-minute timeframe. This way, you will be protected from accessing the markets at the worst moment. The algorithm is able to proceed and track the markets so that you eventually get to find out the best market entry points.

3. Able Trend Trading Platform

This is another platform designed with swing traders in mind. One of its most outstanding features is its ability to identify changes in the trend instantly. Trend direction is first indicated by a distinct color. When the signal is headed upwards, then the color is blue; when it heads downwards, it changes color to red. If there is any sideways movement then the color changes once more to green.

This platform, therefore, makes it pretty easy to observe the market trend and keep abreast with it. Additional information will then enable you to make the necessary trade moves that you need to as a swing trader. For instance, you will notice red and blue dots on your screen. These indicate the various stop points.

When there is a downward trend, then the red dots will indicate your sell points while blue dots will indicate your buy points on the upward trend. These stop points ensure that you partake of the large market movements but with very little risk or exposure.

The reasons why this system is so successful is that it comes with state of the art features. It generates bar and dot colors that you can choose for the different bar charts. These include the 5-minute, 1-minute, daily, tick, and weekly charts. Many traders have termed this platform as both robust and functional. It is a universal platform that can work with different trading systems.

You are able to make large profits if you are able to enter the markets and join the trend at an early stage. Identifying the trend is easy when you have this software. Remember that the trend is a friend of any swing trader. Therefore, spend some time at the beginning of your trades to identify the trend and then move on from here. Identifying the trend at an early stage is what you wish to do. The risks to you are minimal at this stage. This platform helps you identify the trend and provide you with additional crucial information that even large investors do not have.

You are able to operate on any market so that you are not limited to trading stocks only. If you wish to swing trade options, currencies, and other instruments, then you are free to do so. The platform is suitable for all trading styles, including day trading, swing trading, and position trading, and so on.

4. Interactive Brokers

This is a popular platform that has been recently revamped. It is highly rated software because of the useful tools available to traders. Some of these tools are extremely useful for seasoned or sophisticated traders who need more than just the basics.

This platform is able to connect you to any and all exchanges across the world. For instance, you may want to trade markets in Hong Kong, Australia, and so on. The software is able to connect you seamlessly so that you have great trading experience.

This platform has seen the addition of new features which make trading even easier. These are, however, more suitable to seasoned traders who are more sophisticated than the average retail investor or small trader.

One of the attractive features of Interactive Brokers is that it is a very affordable platform to use. It is especially cost-friendly to small scale traders, retail investors, and the ordinary swing trader as the margin rates are low and affordable.

The platform supports trading across 120 markets located in at least 31 countries and deals in more than 23 different currencies. It also supports traders who execute trades pretty fast.

Other Additional Considerations

Before selecting your preferred trading platform, there are certain things that you will have to think about. For instance, what is your account size? In other words, how much funds do you have in your swing trading account? The answer to this question will help you narrow down your choice of platform.

Some platforms are designed for specific financial products like options trading, day trading, currency trading, and swing trading, and so on. As a trader, you should find out if a platform is compatible with your trading style. Therefore, do have the product in mind at all times. Geography is also a consideration is come cases because some platforms are only available to traders in certain jurisdictions and not others.

The strategy is also crucial. As a swing trader, your strategy is to buy and hold for a couple of days or weeks. There are crucial factors that you need to consider, even as you choose a trading platform. For instance, how much automation do you require? Are there any manual functions that are necessary? How about risk management? What kinds of management approach do you desire to cut losses and lock profits? A good level of functionality is definitely necessary.

There is also the issue of cost that you have to consider. As a trader, you can expect to incur some costs. Generally, if you are a regular swing trader trading in stocks, then regular platforms will do just fine. However, should you require something specific such as a personalized platform then you will probably have to pay extra. Try and work with what is readily available rather than finding cool add-ons that may not be necessary at this point in time.

Chapter 4: Different Financial Instruments

There are numerous financial instruments available. A financial instrument signifies a type of contract between two parties. It can be defined as a document that represents a liability to one party and an asset to another. All financial instruments can be legally enforced and contain a monetary value. These financial instruments can be created, traded, and even modified.

Financial instruments can be documents or contracts. Contract documents include stocks, bonds, options, and future. However, they can broadly be classified as either derivative instruments or cash instruments. Derivatives are instruments whose value is derived from the characteristics and value of the underlying instrument. Cash instruments derive their value entirely from the markets. A good example of a cash instrument is a stock or share. These are very easy to liquidate or transfer.

There are plenty of other classifications depending on the type, asset class, and so on. For instance, debt instruments can be classified as either long-term or short-term debts. Others such as Forex-based instruments are in a class of their own.

Stocks

Stocks are the most common type of security that you are likely to come across. These are traded at the stock market, which is a secondary market. Owners or holders of stocks usually trade with willing buyers on a regular basis at the stock exchange. On most occasions, if not all, you will be buying or trading in stocks with other interested participants but not the parent company.

Every stock comes with a quote. This quote is never fixed but varies depending on a number of factors. Prices are not the only information provided. We also have other information available relating to stocks. For instance, traders are interested in volumes traded as the volume is a great indicator of liquidity.

The prices of stocks are often determined through an auction process at the stock exchange. Buyers and sellers basically place bids—and when they coincide, a sale is concluded. If you wish to buy stocks, you will visit your broker who will place bids on your behalf. Alternatively, you can open an online account and do so via a trading platform. Most transactions have moved online, making it easier and more convenient to trade in stocks and shares.

There are different kinds of orders when it comes to the stock market. For instance, we have limit orders and market orders. A market order is where a client uses an online platform or instructs a broker to sell or buy stocks at the best price possible. Market orders never guarantee the price that you want, but you will almost certainly get the number of shares desired.

Limit order simply means an all or none order. In this instance, when you place an order, it will only be fulfilled if you receive the entire amount of shares that you desire. For instance, if you wish to purchase 500 shares of stock ABC, then this AON or all-or-none order will only be fulfilled if the 500 shares are available. If the supply falls short, then the order will not be fulfilled.

We also have what is known as stop orders. In this instance, there will be a contingency placed on a preferred price or amount. You may wish to sell or buy stocks at a certain given price. Once this price is exceeded, then all buying or selling will stop. For instance, if you are buying shares, you may want to purchase at a price not exceeding $50. As long as the stock price remains at or below this price, then the order is met. But once the stock price exceeds $50, the order will stop.

Finally, we also have short selling and margin trading. Margin refers to a loan provided by a broker for trading purposes. When you engage in margin trading, it simply means that you are purchasing stocks using borrowed funds. The same is true when it comes to shares or stocks that do not belong to you. When you sell short, it means that you are selling shares that belong to someone else.

Both margin and short selling are popular with traders. The purpose is always to sell or buy with the aim of buying back or selling with the aim of profiting from the venture. At the same time, you will trade with the hope of returning borrowed stocks or repaying the margin loan.

Stock Indexes

We can define an index as a measure or indicator of a certain parameter. When it comes to financing, the index refers to a measure of the change in a given market. We have stocks, shares, and bonds as securities traded in the financial markets. Some of the popular indexes in the US include the S&P 500 as well as the DJIA or Dow Jones Industrial Average. We also have others, such as the US Aggregate Bond Index. These are often used to benchmark the performance of the US bonds and stock markets, and these are measures of the US economy.

A Closer Look at Indexes

There are different indexes and each related directly to either bonds or stock markets. Also, each index has a specific calculation formula. Usually, the numeric value of an index is not as important as the relative change of the index. The most crucial part to investors is often the total amount an index has fallen or risen with a period of time like 24 hours for instance.

Indexes have a base level of 1,000. However, investors and traders are often interested in the variation of the index from this base level. For instance, if the FTSE 100 has a value of 7643.50, then we can see that it is almost 8 times larger than the base level. As a trader, you need to be on the lookout for the percentage drop or rise of an index.

There is a certain close relationship between exchange-traded funds, mutual funds, and trading indices. Fund managers usually try to mirror certain indexes when they constitute exchange-traded funds and mutual funds. For instance, a fund manager will observe and note all the stocks that constitute a popular index such as the Dow Jones Industrial Average and then mirror that with their fund. This way, the fund will be expected to perform in tandem with the index. Should the index appreciate in value, then the fund will also gain in value.

Because funds such as these mirror major indexes, investors are able to invest in securities contained in an index. The performance of ETFs – electronically traded funds – and mutual funds is often measured by the performance of indexes. Thus they act as benchmarks for investors and traders in most cases. A mutual or ETF fund can compare its returns to that of the S&P 500. This way, investors are able to compare how their fund is performing and whether they are profiting or not in relation to the fund.

One of the most popular indices is the S&P 500 or Standard & Poor's 500. This index is commonly and popularly used by traders, fund managers, investors, and other market players to benchmark the stock market. This index constitutes three quarters or 75% of all the stocks and securities trades across the US.

Another very popular index is the DJIA or the Dow Jones Industrial Average. It is well known, but the only challenge is that it reflects only a small percentage of the stocks traded in the US stock markets. The Dow Jones consists of stocks of no more than 30 companies traded at the stock exchanges. Apart from the DJIA and S&P 500, other notable indexes are Wilshire 5000, NASDAQ, and the Barclays Capital Aggregate Bond Index.

Index funds have been created to enable us to invest indirectly in indexes. We have index funds that track the performance of certain select stocks. A good example of an ETF is the Vanguard S&P 500. It consists of lots of securities that are similar to those found on the S&P 500.

We also have mortgage index funds. ARMs or the Adjustable-Rate Mortgages constitute adjustable interest rates that last throughout the lifetime of the mortgage. This rate is basically determined through the use of a margin that is added to an index. A good example of an ARM is LIBOR or London Interbank Offer Rate. To determine the interest on a loan, all you need to do is determine the LIBOR rate and mortgage index to the LIBOR. If the former is 3% and the latter is 2%, then the interest rate on a mortgage is3%-2% = 1%.

Trading Forex

Currencies from across the world are traded at the Forex markets. In fact, the Forex market is the most liquid market. The reason for this is that all transactions are opened and closed using cash and trades are concluded instantly. There are trillions of dollars in circulation each day with traders located in countries all around the world. The most amazing part is that there are no central authorities that oversee the Forex market. This is a self-regulating market. It consists of a network of individual traders, banks, other institutions, and brokers. All trades are executed via banks and brokers.

If you wish to trade in currencies, then you will first have to learn how to trade. Once you are confident about your trading skills, you can then begin trading. The Forex markets are accessible and every single business day 24 hours a day throughout the year. Sometimes, Forex trading is available even during the holidays when it is made available in other jurisdictions. For instance, there may be a US national holiday such as Memorial Day. Currency trading may still be available through other countries where they do not have a similar holiday.

There are numerous companies that deal in Forex. Such companies often trade with clients or customers overseas. Currency fluctuations affect their businesses, especially when they buy or sell products and services. Hedging against currency options is one way of countering the challenge posed by fluctuations. This is achievable through Forex markets.

Forex is traded in pairs and offered as a quote. Currency pairs' examples include USD/JPY, CAD/AUS, and so on. A quote that is offered on a currency pair refers to the ratio of the value of one currency against the other. For instance, if we have the currency pair USD/CAD quoted as 1.2569, then it means that one US dollar has a value equivalent to 1.2569 CAD. As such, it costs 1.2569 CAD to buy 1 USD. These values are never static but dynamic and constantly changing because of different reasons.

Trading the Forex markets is easy and straight forward. It is very similar to trading stocks. The only difference, in this case, is the financial instrument. If you can trade stocks, then you should be able to adjust to trading Forex because the principle is the same. When you trade in Forex, you are actually buying currencies. It is what a tourist from France, for instance, would do with their euros in the US. They would exchange them for US dollars.

Options Trading

Options are a versatile product for trade and investment. They can be defined as derivative contracts where buys have a right but not obligation to purchase underlying security. The underlying security is usually priced at an agreed amount. While the buyer of an option is under no obligation to buy the underlying security, the seller is always obligated to sell should the buyer exercise their right.

Both investors and traders sell and buy options. Sometimes, investors and business owners buy options for hedging purposes. This means that they buy options to reduce their risks regarding exposure. However, most traders and investors sell and buy options to generate an income, earn a profit, growth their investments, and so on.

Options trading can be very lucrative because profitability is exponentially, unlike with other instruments. You could easily make over ten or even twenty times of your capital with just a single trade. However, options are also a very risky prospect. A lot of traders lose money trying to trade options. Ensure that you only do so if you are skilled, experienced, and have a sure trading plan.

When you sell options, you get to earn fees. Writing options can be a simple way of making an income. There is also the advantage of leverage when trading options as well as protection of a portfolio by hedging. Therefore, trading options can be very rewarding and fulfilling.

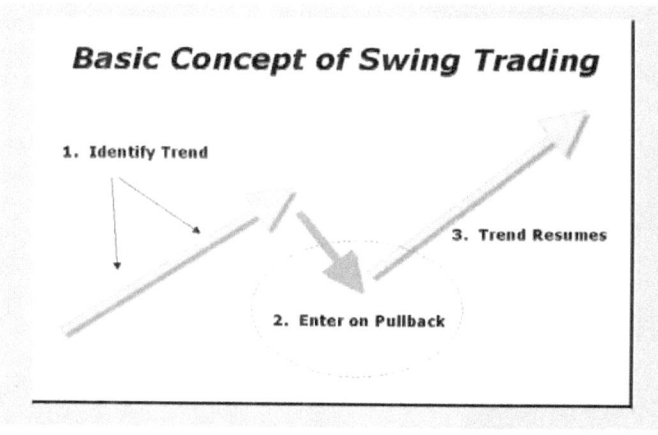

Chapter 5: Risk Assessment and Management

Risk management is a deliberate action taken by a trader or investor. The purpose is to keep losses at a minimum. As a trader, you are exposed to a lot of dangers. You can lose money if you are not careful or if your strategy was not successful. Should you lose money in a trade, then the risk can be managed. All that you need to do is to open yourself up to being profitable in the market.

Most traders are unaware of risk management yet it is a crucial aspect of any serious trader. If you wish to make money in the markets for the long term, then risk management is absolutely essential. Even if you are a great trader and profitable most of the time, your profits can be wiped out in a matter of seconds without proper risk management.

Risk assessment can be defined as a general term that measures the chances of the likelihood of incurring losses when trading. It is also applicable in other areas such as investments, owning an asset, and so much more. Risk management also helps to realize the required rate of return so that a strategy becomes successful.

As a trader, you really need to incorporate risk management as part of your trading strategy. There are a number of different approaches to risk management, so it is advisable to consider the approach that best works for you.

Plan Your Trades

The single most crucial aspect of your trade should be risk management. Without it, your whole trading life will be in jeopardy. Therefore, start all your trading ventures with a plan that you intend to stick by. Traders have a saying that you should plan your trades and then trade your plan. This means to come up with the best plan possible and then implement it and stick by it. Trade is very similar to war. When it is well planned, it can be won before it is executed.

Some of the best tools you will need as part of your risk management plan are take-profit and stop-loss. Using these two tools, you can plan your trades in advance. You will need to use technical analysis in order to determine these two points. With this information, you should be able to determine the price you are willing to pay as well as the losses you can incur.

The One Percent Rule

Traders often apply what is known as the one percent rule. This rule dictates that you should not risk amounts greater than one percent of your total trading capital on one single trade. For instance, if you have $15,000 as your trading capital, then you should never risk more than $150 on a single trade. This is a great risk management approach that you can use as part of your trading strategy. Usually, most traders who adopt this strategy have amounts less than $100,000 in their trading accounts. There are some who are so more confident, so they choose to work with 2% instead.

Setting Target and Stops

We can define a stop-loss as the total amount of loss that a trader is willing to incur in a single trade.

Beyond the stop-loss point, the trader exits the trade. This is basically meant to prevent further losses by thinking the trade will eventually get some momentum. We also have what is known as a take-profit point. It is at this point that you will collect any profits made and possibly exit a trade. At this point, a particular stock or other security is often very close to the point of resistance. Beyond this point, a reversal in price is likely to take place. Rather than lose money, you should exit the trade. Traders sometimes take profit and let a particular trade continue if it was still making money. Another take-profit point is then plotted. If you have a good run, you are allowed to lock in the profits and let the good run continue.

Moving Averages

The best way to identify these two crucial points is to use moving averages. The reason why we prefer moving averages is to determine the stop-loss and take-profit points. These are closely tracked by the markets and very simple to determine. Some of the popular moving averages include the 5-day, 20-day, 50-day, 100-day, and 200-day averages. Simply apply these to your security's chart then make a determination about the best points.

You can also use support and resistance lines to determine the take-profit and stop-loss points. This is also a pretty simple process. Simply connect past lows and highs that happened in the recent past on key, high-than-normal volume levels. They work on the same principle as the moving averages. All that you need to do is to find levels where the price action will respond to the trend line on areas of high volume.

Assessing Risk versus Reward

A lot of traders lose a lot of money at the markets for a very simple reason. They do not know about risk management or how to go about it. This mostly happens to beginners or novice traders. Most of them simply learn how to trade then rush to the markets in the hope of making a kill. Sadly, this is now how things work because account and risk management are not taken into consideration.

Managing risk is just as important as learning how to trade profitably. It is a skill that every trader needs to learn including beginners and novice traders. As it is, investing hard-earned funds at the markets can be a risky venture. Even with the very best techniques and latest software programs, you can still lose money. Experts also lose money at the markets occasionally. The crucial aspect is that they win a lot more than they lose, so the net equation is profitability.

Since trading is a risky affair, traders should be handsomely compensated for the risks they take. This is where the term risk vs. reward ratio comes in. If you are going to invest your money in a venture that carries some risk, then it is good to understand the nature of the risk. If it is too risky, then you may want to keep away but if not, then perhaps the risk is worth it.

Think about it this way. Supposing someone you don't trust many approaches you for a $1,000 loan with a promise to pay you back with $100 interest after a month. You may be hesitant because the risk is greater compared than the profit. However, if he promises to pay you back after one month with a $2,000 interest, then the risk is well worth it. The ratio of risk versus reward, in this case, is 2:1. A lot of investors believe this to be an excellent ratio and many would take it because they get a chance to double their money. If the borrower offered to pay back $3,000, then the risk vs. reward ratio increases to 3:1.

This same process also applies to the stock market and to other financial markets. Let's assume you have selected stock ABC to trade at the stock market. The stock price is down to $20 from a recent high of $25. According to your informed assessment, this price should rise to previous highs of $25 in the near future.

You decide to invest about $500 of your funds on this trade. This amount buys you 25 shares of ABC stock. If you did your assessment and analysis correctly, then you stand a chance of making money and with the capacity to limit losses. In this case, you can choose the value of $25 as the upper limit where you cease trading and first take profits. This is also known as the take profit point.
You can then choose the value of $17 as your stop loss. This means that in case the price drop to $17, then you will automatically exit the trade and count your losses. The maximum loss you can incur on this trade

is $3 ($20-$17) * 20 shares = $60. On the other hand, the maximum profitability in our case would be $5 ($25 - $20) * 20 = $100. So with this trade, you stand to gain $100 or lose $60. As such, the risk versus reward ratio is 100:60 or 1:0.6 which is close to 2:1. This ratio is considered acceptable even though it is the minimum acceptable risk versus reward ratio.

Steps to Determine a Suitable Risk vs. Reward Ratio

1. First, identify the most appropriate stock or other security to trade. Make sure that you conduct exhaustive and thorough research in order to identify the most appropriate security.

2. Next, determine the upside point as well as the downside points. The upside is where you take profit before a reversal while the downside is where you exit a trade to prevent further losses. Use the current price to make these determinations.

3. Now, determine the risk versus reward ratio. Have a threshold for this and do not take anything below your threshold. Most traders prefer ratios starting at

4:1 even though 2:1 is considered the minimum ratio for any trade. In case your ratio is insufficient, then raise your stop-loss levels to acceptable levels.

Always ensure to apply the risk versus reward ratio for all your trades. Keep in mind the indicated acceptable levels. If you are unable to find acceptable ratios after trying several times, find another security. Once you learn how to incorporate risk management into your trades, you will become safer as you trade without incurring any huge losses.

Optimum Trade Size

As a trader, you also need to make determinations regarding other aspects of the trade. These include the number of stock or currency or any other financial markets' instruments. When doing this, most traders overlook position size. They feel like it is not important enough or sometimes they have no clue that it is necessary and how to determine an optimum one.

There are certain acceptable ways of going through with this. The first step is usually determining the "stop level." This is the point at which we intend to take a break from trading and consolidate our gains. If the stock continues with its bullish run, then we can let it continue but as long as we keep setting profit-take points and stop-loss points.

Once the stop-loss point is determined, we can then proceed to determine our risk levels. It is only after having all this information that we will then be able to come up with the position size or trade size. We also need to examine our trading account size to determine the size of our trades. Basically, small scale traders and retail investors should invest between 1% and 3% of their account size into one single trade.

Take the example of a trading account with amounts of $10,000. Then, in this case, you will only risk about $100 per trade and no more. If you were to trade the stocks market, then you could choose to buy stocks worth no more than $100 to fulfill this trade.

Some traders have large accounts and wish they could spend freely. These usually employ different approaches when it comes to position size. Even if you had an account worth $500,000, then you would not want to risk over $500 per trade. This is equivalent to 1% of the total amount in the account.

Sometimes, people choose stop levels for the day. These are daily stop orders issued by a client to their broker and so on. Daily stop-loss points simply indicate the amount of money that you are ready to lose per trade. Should this level be attained as you trade, then you will have to stop trading and exit all other possible positions in the market.

Experienced traders usually opt to equate the daily stop-loss positions as equivalent to their average profitability. So if a person makes $400, then their stop loss order will be a lot closer to this figure.

Maintaining a Trade Journal

As a trader, you need to keep a journal so that you have a reliable record of your trades and their performance. This is one of the best ways of learning about your style and performance. Trade tracking journals also enables you to track your trades and the actions you took during certain situations and instances. In short, a trading journal provides traders with the necessary tools and information that they need to evaluate their trading activities objectively.

As a trader, you really should be tracking your trades throughout the day. A journal helps you to keep a record of the happenings each day as well as your reactions or actions. Your plan should include a tried and tested system that suits your trading style. Make sure that you test this system and review it often then improve your trading plans and performance.

Poor trading systems do not necessarily cause failure or bad performance. Most traders lose out and incur losses simply because they do not adhere to the rules of their preferred trading system. Many lose out because they cannot keep track of their trading plan. This is where a trade journal comes in handy.

If you have a serious trading plan, then a journal will help you to adhere to this trading plan. By following you well laid out plan, you will have much better chances of success. It is important to keep the journal as detailed as possible. Here are some of the ways you can make your journal as thorough as possible. This is important as your journal is only as good as the information it contains.

First, you need to ensure that that you are honest with the information you enter and as thorough as possible. It beats the purpose is the information provided is not accurate and honest because it will be of very little benefit to you. Also, you should learn how to enter information and data into a trading journal and how to maintain it appropriately. This way, you will become a disciplined trader.

Also, with time, you should begin reflecting on your journal entries. When you do this, you will learn a lot about yourself, and you will improve your trading skills immensely. You also get to track your thoughts and trades the entire trading day.

Tips on Maintaining a Trading Journal

A trading journal contains useful information and relevant details that what you receive from your broker as your trading performance. You will get to learn more about market conditions prevalent during your trading experiences. If you made any mistakes as you were trading or got distracted somewhat, then the journal will be able to keep track of any errors and mistakes. You can also put down any trading strategy that may come up in the course of trading.

Ensure that you put down as much detail as possible. For instance, remember to include the prevailing market conditions at the time the trade was underway. The entries will open up your eyes to plenty of things that traders miss as they trade. A journal may not be so crucial to a day trader but is definitely recommended for all swing traders.

It is advisable to note that there is no need to actually take a pen and notebook and physically enter every minute detail that occurs. Instead, you can use other preferred methods. For instance, we could use regular screen captures to take a picture of the trading platform as the trade progresses.

Other swing traders prefer to add notes, marks, and annotations to their trading charts in the course of the trading day. They mark indicator levels and draw lines. These actions are useful in a number of ways and can help in determining the direction of the trend. It also helps when it comes to identifying possible entry points and reversal points. Charts indicate the exact market conditions during the entire trading day. Many find it easy to keep pictures of different instances of the trading day. However, notes here and there, marks, and annotations help to make things clear.

Marking Charts

Marking charts is pretty simple and straightforward. However, there are a few basic guidelines that you need to follow. These guidelines make your charts easier to read and understand later on.

First, make sure that you have at least an hour and possibly even two of the price action prior to the start of your trading day. This way, you will be able to have an idea and context of activities just before your trading day started. You will be able to assess the various time frames a lot better.

Make sure to include or indicate any major economic and financial events that may have taken place. For instance, were there any financial reports released, earnings reports? Then these can be noted down. Also, note down that you were not necessarily trading because of the news.

Ensure to keep as many drawings and trend lines as possible on your timeline. Make sure that they do not distract you or get in your way. The drawings and trend lines will make it easy for you when you want to view your previous trading sessions and your performance then.

Make sure that you also include the total number of trades that you had in one single trading day. Include the number of fails and number of successes so you can know which approach works and which approach was not successful. Also, include the dates whenever you save a chart. You can use the date as the file name and store all trading files in a single folder.

Review Your Trading Journal Regularly

A trading journal is an essential tool for any serious swing trader hoping to be profitable in the long term. If you do so, then within a period of about a month only, you will begin noticing a pattern forming. You can use this journal as a learning tool to help open your eyes to things nobody will ever teach you about trading.

Take time at the end of each trading week to review your performance and how you fared. Also review the journal once each month, preferably at the end of the month. See where your strengths and weaknesses lie and then note any common problems—if you notice the strengths that you have, then see how you can maintain the momentum here. Also, notice your weaknesses and plan on doing better in those areas.

Capturing your trading information is more effective when you take screenshots rather than collecting necessary information and writing it down on paper. Also, if you prefer writing anything down, you can do so on the charts for easy reference in the future. It is also possible to have a written journal if you prefer. It is also advisable to have digital records as these are easier to obtain and keep.

Finally, remember that your trading journal, whether paper or digital is an invaluable learning tool that you need to improve your trades. It provides an excellent mechanism in training your mind and eyes to see a lot of things, including setups that will aid you when trading.

Chapter 6: Fundamental Analysis

If you want to be a successful stock trader, a swing trader, or an analyst, then you have to learn about fundamental analysis. It is the most crucial aspect of any investment or trading strategy. Many would claim that a trader is not really accomplished if they do not perform fundamental analysis.

The fact is that fundamental analysis is such a broad subject that what it entails sometimes differs depending on scope and strategy. It involves a lot of things such as regulatory filings, financial statements, valuation techniques, and so on.

Definition

Fundamental analysis can be defined as the examination, investigation, and research into the underlying factors that closely affect the financial health, success, and wellbeing of companies, industries, and the general economy.

It can also be defined as a technique used by traders and investors to make a determination regarding the value of a stock or any other financial instrument by examining the factors that directly and indirectly affect a company's or industry's current and future business, financial, economic prospects.

At its most generic form, fundamental analysis endeavors to predict and learn the intrinsic value of securities such as stocks. An in-depth examination and analysis of certain financial, economic, quantitative, and qualitative factors will help in providing the solution.

Fundamental analysis is mostly performed on a company so a trader can determine whether or not to deal in its stocks. However, it can also be performed on the general economy and on particular industries such as the motor industry, energy sector, and so on.

Basics of Fundamental Analysis

The main purpose of fundamental analysis is to receive a forecast and thereby profit from future price movements. There are certain questions that fundamental analysis seeks to answer. For instance, an analyst or swing trader may wish to know answers to the following questions;

- ☐ Is the firm's revenue growing?
- ☐ Is it profitable in both the short and long terms?
- ☐ Can if afford to settle its liabilities?
- ☐ Can it outsmart its competitors?
- ☐ Is the company's outlook genuine or fraudulent?

These are just a few examples of the numerous questions that fundamental analysis seeks to answer. Sometimes, traders also want answers to questions not mentioned above. In short, therefore, the purpose is to obtain and profit from expected price movements in the short-to-near-term future.

Most of the fundamental analysis is conducted at a company level because traders and investors are mostly interested in information that will enable them to make a decision at the markets. They want information that will guide them in selecting the most suitable stocks to trade at the markets. As such, traders and investors searching for stocks to trade will resort to examining the competition, a company's business concept, its management, and financial data.

For a proper forecast regarding future stock prices, a trader is required to take into consideration a company's analysis, industry analysis, and even the overall economic outlook. This way, a trader will be able to determine the latest stock price as well as predicted future stock price. When the outcome of fundamental analysis is not equal to the current market price, then it means that the stock is overpriced or perhaps even undervalued.

Steps to Fundamental Evaluation

There is basically no clear-cut pathway or method of conducting fundamental analysis. However, we can break down the entire process so that you know exactly where to begin. The most preferred approach is the top-down approach. We begin by examining the general economy followed by industry group before finally ending with the company in question. In some instances, though, the bottom-up approach is also used.

Companies are often compared with others. For instance, we may want to compare energy companies Exxon Mobil and British Petroleum. However, we cannot compare companies in different industries. For instance, we cannot compare a financial company like City Group with a technology firm like Google.

Determine the Stock or Security

You need first to have a stock or security in mind. There are many factors that determine the stocks to trade. For instance, you may want to target blue-chip companies noted for exemplary stock market performance, profitability, and stability. You also want to focus on companies that constitute one of the major indices such as the Dow Jones Industrial Average or S&P 500. The stocks should have large trading volumes for purposes of liquidity.

Economic Forecast

The overall performance of the economy basically affects all companies. Therefore, when the economy fares well, then it follows that most companies will succeed. This is because the economy is like a tide while the various companies are vessels directed by the tide.

There is a general correlation between the performance of companies and their stocks and the performance of the general economy. The economy can also be narrowed to focus on specific sectors. For instance, we have the energy sector, transport sector, manufacturing, hospitality, and so on. Narrowing down to specific sectors is crucial for proper analysis.

There are certain factors that we need to consider when looking at the general economy. We have the market size, growth rate, and so on. Basically, when stocks move in the markets, they tend to move as a group. This is because when a sector does well, then most companies in that sector will also excel.

Company Analysis

One of the most crucial steps in fundamental analysis is company analysis. At this stage, you will come up with a compiled shortlist of companies. Different companies have varying capabilities and resources. The aim in our case is to find companies that can develop and keep a competitive advantage over its competitors and others in the same market. Some of the factors that are looked into at this stage include sound financial records, a solid management team, and a credible business plan.

When it comes to companies, the best approach is to check out a company's qualitative aspects, followed by quantitative before checking out its financial outlook. We shall begin with the qualitative aspect of the company analysis. One of the most crucial is the company's business model.

Business Model

One of the most crucial questions that analysts and all others ask about a company is what it does exactly. This is a simple yet fundamental question. A company's business model is simply what the company does to make money. The best way to learn about a company's business model is to visit its website and learn more about what it does. You can also check out its 10-K filings to find out more.

You need to make sure that you thoroughly understand the business model of each and every company that you invest in. Most companies have very simple business models. Take MacDonald's for instance. They sell hamburgers and fries. At other times it is not easy to understand what a company does. For instance, the world's best-known investor, Warren Buffet, does not invest in tech companies because he simply doesn't understand what they do.

Competitive Advantage

We also need to take a closer look at a company's competitive advantage. Any company that is to survive the long term needs to have a competitive edge over its competitors. A company with one such advantage has to be Coca Cola because of the unique nature of their products. Others are Microsoft, Toyota, and Google. Their business models provide them with a competitive edge that is hard for others to compete with.

In general, a unique competitive edge is where a company has clear trade-offs and options for customers compared to competitors, a unique product or service, reliable operational effectiveness and a great fit in all activities.

Management

Also crucial for any serious company is its management. Any company worth its salt has to have top quality management in major positions. Investors and analysts usually look at the level and quality of management to determine their competences, experience, strengths, and capabilities. This is because they hold in their hands the fate of a company. Even a great company with excellent ideas and plans can fail if the management is not right.

It is advisable to find out how qualified, experienced, successful, and committed the leadership of a company is. For instance, do they have prior experience at senior levels? Is there a track record and can management deliver on its stated objectives? These are crucial questions that should be answered appropriately for a positive conclusion.

There are plenty of tools available to the ordinary investor to learn more about a publicly traded company's management. One of these is the company's website. Such a site is a trove of information regarding top managers such as the chief officers. You can also check out the conference calls where company C-suite executives host press conferences and present quarterly earnings reports. Many analysts await such opportunities to ask any questions they may have.

We also have the management discussion and analysis sessions that take place at the start of annual reports. During these instances, top managers often speak candidly about the company's future outlook and things like that. Also, watch out for corporate governance. This has to do with a company's guidelines and policies in place. It refers to the relationship that a company has with the management, stakeholders, and directors. You can find these guidelines and policies in the company's charter.

Effective corporate governance occurs where companies are able to adhere to their charters as well as all applicable federal and local regulations. Other factors that you should watch out for include the structure and constitution of the board of directors, the rights of all stakeholders, transparency and financial information, and so on.

Industry Factors

When conducting your company analysis, there are other factors that you will need to consider here. These factors include business cycles, the competition, growth in the industry, government regulation, and others. It is advisable also to have an understanding of the workings of a specific industry that you are interested in.

You should endeavor to learn more about the customer served by the said industry. There are companies that have millions of customers, while others serve only a handful. A company that relies solely on a tiny number of customers for its revenue is considered a negative position and a red flag. However, companies with a large customer base stand a much better chance of doing well if they sell to millions of customers across the board. Therefore, a firm with a large customer base is rated highly compared with one that sells to only a handful of buyers.

Government Policy

In countries such as the United States, government policy is extremely crucial. When conducting fundamental analysis, you really should take this into perspective because certain policies can completely kill an industry. Companies provide relevant information on their 10-K forms which you can always look into.

Market Share

Different companies within the same industry sometimes have to work hard to gain market share. There are sometimes a lot of companies fighting for a small share of customers, especially at a local level. If a company controls about 85% of the market, then it means it is a solid company with strong fundamentals.

A strong market share also means that a company possesses that competitive edge over its customers. It also means that the company is larger than its rivals and hence has a great future outlook.

Industry Growth

This is also another aspect that should be taken into account. Some companies may have everything else working for them, but future growth prospects may not be so bright. It is important to assess an industry and confirm whether there are any prospects for future growth.

Fundamental Analysis Example

One of the world's best known and most successful stock analysts is Mr. Warren Buffet. He uses fundamental analysis to determine which shares to buy and which companies to invest in. His success as an analyst has turned him into a billionaire.

Apart from analyzing companies, the equities market can also be analyzed. There are some analysts who conducted a fundamental analysis of the S&P 500 for a period of a week. This was from 4th July to 8th July 2016. Within this period of time, the S&P index went up to 2129.90 following the release of an impressive jobs report within the US. This was an unprecedented performance surpassed only by the May 2015 which was 2132.80. The superb performance was attributed to the announcement of 287,000 new jobs across the country.

What Does "Fundamental" Refer to?

When we talk of fundamentals, we actually mean the quantitative and qualitative data that significantly contributes to the success and financial valuation of a company. It also includes an assessment of both macroeconomics and microeconomics aspects. These are aspects that are essential for determining the worth of a company or other assets.

Microeconomics and Macroeconomics

Macroeconomics stands for all factors that affect the general economy. These are factors such as inflation, supply and demand, unemployment and even GDP growth. They also include international trade and prevailing monetary and fiscal policies put forth by the authorities. Macroeconomic considerations are useful when it comes to matters of large-scale analysis of the economy and how these relate to business activities.

Microeconomic factors are those that focus on the smaller elements of the economy. These include elements in certain particular sectors of a market—for example, labor issues in a given market, matters such as supply and demand, and others such as labor and consumer issues relating to the said industry.

Stock Analysis

Stock analysis can be defined as the process used by traders and investors to acquire in-depth information about a stock or company. The analysis is done by evaluating and studying current and past data about the stock or even company. This way, traders and investors are able to gain a significant edge in the market as they will be in a position to make well-informed decisions.

Technical Analysis Versus Fundamental Analysis

When analyzing a stock, analysts usually perform both fundamental and technical analysis. Fundamental analysis relies mostly on different sources of data such as economic reports, financial records, market share, and company assets. For publicly listed companies, the data is usually sourced from financial statements such as cash flow statements, income statements, footnotes, and balance sheet.

Such information is readily available to the public via 10-K and 10-Q reports. You can access the reports via the EDGAR database system that is managed by the SEC or Securities and Exchange Commission. Data can also be sourced from companies' earnings reports, which are often released quarterly.

Fundamental Analysis

Some of the parameters that analysts look at within a company's financial statement include a measure of solvency, profitability, liquidity, growth trajectory, efficiency, and leverage. Analysts also use rations to work out the financial health of companies. Examples of such ratios include quick ratio and current ratio. These rations are useful in determining a company's ability to repay short-term liabilities based on their current assets.

To find the current ratio, you will divide the current assets with the current liabilities. These figures can easily be accessed from the company's balance sheet. While there is no ratio that is considered ideal, anything below 1 is considered a poor financial situation that is incapable of meeting all short-term debts.

The balance sheet also provides analysts with additional information such as current debt amounts owed by the company. In such a situation, the analysis will focus on the debt ratio. This is computed by working out all the liabilities and dividing by the total assets. When the ratio is computed, a ratio greater than 1.0 does point to a company with a lot more debt compared to its assets. This means that in case the interest rates rise, then the firm may default on its debts.

The stock analysis involves not just current financial reports but also compares the current financial statements with those from previous years. This will give a trader or investor a feel of the company's performance and will determine whether the firm is stable, receding, or growing. It is also common for an analyst to compare a company's financial statement with those of other companies in the same sector. This is done in order to compare profitability and other parameters.

Of great importance is the operating profit. It is a measure of the revenue that a company is left with after other expenses have been cleared. Basically, a firm with operating margins of 0.27 is favorably viewed when compared with one whose margin is

0.027, for instance. This can be translated to mean that the firm whose operating margin is 0.27 spends 73 cents per dollar earned to foot its operating costs.

Financial Statements

Fundamental analysis at a company level would be incomplete with analyzing the company's financial performance. There is often more than one financial document available. In fact, most companies produce or generate numerous financial statements that it becomes difficult to understand them all. Most often, they present investors with a huge challenge. However, with a little bit of information and exposure, you can understand these financial documents. This is advisable because they contain a wealth of information.

The Balance Sheet

Financial statements are actually financial documents that provide information regarding a company's performance. One of the major documents necessary for financial analysis is the balance sheet. This financial document is referred to as the balance sheet because all assets stated therein must balance with all liabilities.

Assets include all the different resources such as property, machinery, and money that a company owns or controls at a given time. Liabilities are all the items that a company owes others. These include items such as debts, loans, and so on. Liabilities are often summed up together with equity. Equity refers to the total capital put together by founders of the company as well as shareholders. A company needs to be able to pay off its liabilities, generate returns for shareholders, and still remain profitable and viable in the long run.

The Income Statement

Another crucial financial document is the company's income statement. This is a statement that paints a clear picture of a company's performance in a certain period of time. We generally have income statements on a quarterly and annual basis, but it is possible to have one every single month.

The information contained in income statements helps analysts and others to learn more about the expenses, revenues, and profits generated in the course of a given trading period.

Cash Flow Statements

Also of great importance to investors is the cash flow statement. Basically, a cash flow statement informs us of the monies that a company gained and the amounts that were spent. Companies generally experience both cash inflows and outflows. There needs to be a balance such that the cash that comes into a company's coffers is more than that which is made as payments to others.

Components of cash flow statements include daily cash flows or operating cash flows, cash from investing, and cash from financing. Business can hardly manipulate their financial situations, especially when it comes to cash. As such, this is a crucial statement when examining or analyzing the financial position of a company.

Clever accountants can achieve much, and sometimes, they do get creative in their reporting. However, when it comes to cash, especially liquid cash, they cannot apply any underhand tactics. It is not possible, for instance, to fake cash in the bank. This is one of the reasons why most investors and analysts prefer looking at cash flow statements more than anything else.

We have talked about three different financial documents. These are the balance sheet, income statement, and cash flow statement. As a trader, you need to know where to find these. There are several places wherein these can be found. In the USA, we can find these on the 10Q and 10K filings. These are often filed with the SEC on a quarterly and annual basis, respectively.

You can also find these documents in the annual reports released by businesses. Most people refer to these as 10-K reports. These documents contain all the necessary information often found in the financial reports, including the three documents mentioned above.

Summary

If you are thinking about investing in a company or trading its shares, then you need to ensure that you completely understand as much as possible about the company. This means understanding what it does exactly, its current performance, future outlook, corporate policy, management, and so much more. It is considered a really bad practice to blindly invest in a company whose fundamentals you do not know.

There are numerous things to watch out for when researching a company. However, the single most crucial document is the financial statement. You need to examine a company's financial statements in order to receive a true picture of its performance and future outlook. Ensure that you can understand and interpret the information contained in these statements.

As it is publishing of financial statements is a legal requirement for all publicly traded companies. The most common documents are published quarterly and also annually. To get insights into the thoughts of top management, including C-suite executives, then the

MD&A sessions or management discussions and analysts provide an excellent platform. You can listen to executives discuss pertinent issues and provide their strategies and plans regarding the companies they run.

It is much better to focus on audited reports rather than unaudited ones. The former is a lot more credible compared to the latter. Balance sheets constitute a financial statement that summarizes a company's assets, liabilities, and equity. Income statements, on the other hand, contain figures indicating earnings, expenses, revenue, and earnings per share. Remember to read closely the notes contained in the financial reports for a deeper understanding of various figures within the reports.

Chapter 7: Technical Analysis

Technical analysis can be defined simply as a method, process, or tool that is used by traders to predict and foretell a stock's price movement based on data from the markets.

We can also define technical analysis of trends and stocks as the analysis of past market data that includes volume and price. The main purpose of the analysis is to obtain information that helps in predicting expected market behavior. Traders and investors believe strongly that precious stock price is a reliable indicator of future performance.

There is a notion that supports technical analysis. Apparently, selling and purchase of stocks at the markets collectively by traders, investors, and other players is accurately manifested in the security. This holds then that technical analysis provides a fair and relative accurate market price to a stock or any other security.

Purpose of Technical Analysis

The main purpose of technical analysis is to foretell the expected price movements of stocks and trends and to provide relevant information to investors, traders, and other market players so they can trade profitably.

As a swing trader, you will apply technical analysis to the various charts that you will be using. You will use different tools on the charts so as to determine what the potential entry and exit points for a particular trade are.

Factors Affecting Technical Analysis

Technical analysis can be applied to numerous securities, including Forex, stocks, futures, commodities, indices, and many more. The price of a security depends on a collection of metrics. These are volume, low, open, high, close, open interest, and so on. These are also known as market action or price data.

There are a couple of assumptions that we make as traders when performing technical analysis. However, remember that it is applicable only in situations where the price is only a factor of demand and supply. Should there be other factors that can influence prices significantly, then the technical analysis will not work. The following assumptions are often made about securities that are being analyzed.

There are no artificial price movements: Artificial price movements are usually as a result of distributions, dividends, and splits. Such changes in stock price can greatly alter the price chart, and this tends to cause technical analysis to be very difficult to implement. Fortunately, it is possible to remedy this. All that you need to do as an analyst is to make adjustments to historical data before the price changes.

The stock is highly liquid: Another major assumption that technical analysis makes is that the stock is highly liquid. Liquidity is absolutely crucial for volumes. When stocks are heavily traded as a result of liquidity and volume, then traders are able to enter and exit trades easily. Stocks that are not highly traded tend to be rather difficult to trade because there are very few sellers and buyers at any point in time. Also, stocks with low liquidity are usually poorly priced, sometimes at less than a penny for each share. This is risky as they can be manipulated by investors.

Examine the Charts

Experts advise that traders closely examine the chart of the stock they intend to buy as part of the technical analysis. When you examine the charts, you will be looking to spot the bottom and identify the best entry points. You will also examine the ceiling in order to identify the ideal exit points. All investors purchase stocks hoping the price will almost immediately go up. It is, therefore, crucial to look at and understand historical chart patterns of the particular stock.

The buy point can be looked at as the ground floor of a building where an elevator is about to rise to new highs. You do not only buy the right stock at the right price but also at the right time.

Cup with Handle Pattern

One of the most powerful patterns that allow consistency with stock purchase is the *cup with handle* pattern. This is the point where you buy a stock at its lowest price and is likely to rise very fast. Human nature is still the same where traders and other players in the markets exhibit either greed or fear.

What is "Buy Point?"

This is defined as the price level where a stock is very likely to rise significantly. The buy point, also known as an entry point, is a point in the chart that offers the least resistance to a price increase.

Example:
Cup without a handle is an approach that has worked over centuries. It is still believed to among the most successful strategies for determining entry points. Let us take a stock that has seen its price decline by up to 33%. This is after a successful upward trend that showcased an all-time high.

However, for 6 weeks, the stock starts to decline. However, once the decline is over and the upward trend begins, there are no signs of a major pullback. At this level, the entry point is pretty simple to determine. It is identified to be 10 cents on top of the peak towards the left-hand side—as soon as the stock recovers and gains 10 cents on top of the previous highest level. It is at this point that you enter the trade.

Past Price a Reliable Indicator of Future Performance

Traders understand basically that past price action of a particular stock and most other securities can help to predict the future performance of the same stock accurately. This is why traders are always researching and analyzing the past performance of various securities.

There are lots of other financial experts who rely on technical analysis and not just swing traders. We have analysts, investors, mutual fund managers, finance companies and others who use fundamental analysis followed by technical analysis thereafter. Technical analysis enables all these experts to narrow down to reliable, minimal risk entry price levels.

Charting Varying Time Frames

Future price movement is accurately predicted using charts. There are different kinds of charts available with respect to a single security. There is the 5-minute chart and the 15-minute chart then there are the 1-hour and the 4-hour charts and finally the daily chart.

There are primarily two variables at play when it comes to chart and technical analysis. These are the particular technical indicators and the time frames mentioned above. Oftentimes, the timeframe that was chosen by traders reflects their personal trading style preferences. We have different kinds of traders from intra-day traders, to day traders, swing traders, long-term traders, and investors, among others.

How to Read Charts

There are numerous types of stock charts. Examples of these charts include candlestick charts, line charts, point-and-figure, open-high-low-close charts, bar charts, and many others. These charts are viewable in varying time frames. For instance, we have weekly, daily, intraday, and even monthly charts.

There are advantages and downsides of each chart type and time frame. They find application in different situations. What they reveal include price and volume action, which are extremely important to traders and investors.

Why Are Stock Charts Valuable?

When you find a share that you think has strong fundamentals, the next step is to its charts. The stock chart will provide you with useful insights that will guide you on the best time to enter a trade, how long to stay in the trade and when to exit.

Charts often plot both volume and price data in a format that is easy to read. This way, you can easily spot entry and exit points. Therefore, volume and price are the key metrics to look out for.

Stock Chart Interpretation

Price

On the stock chart above, there are magenta and blue colored marks. These marks represent the stock's price history. The volumes are also represented on the chart. The bars represent the price. The length of the vertical bars on the charts indicates a stock's price range. Therefore, the top of the bar indicates the highest price paid in that specific time period, while the bottom of the bar indicates the lowest stock price paid.

The tiny intersecting lines horizontally running point to the closing price at the end of the particular trading period. When the bar is in blue, this implies that stock price is equal to or greater than the previous price. However, it will be represented by magenta color if it is less than the previous price.

Volumes

At the bottom of the chart are vertical lines. These vertical lines represent the volume of shares trades within the indicated period of time. The height of the volume bars represents a value that is similar to that indicated on the right-hand side scale.

The color of the bars is determined by the preceding price bar. The bar color is blue if the price is greater than or equal to the previous period's last price. The color is magenta if the price is lower than in the previous period's final price.

Moving Averages

Moving averages are indicated on stock charts in order to smooth out price data through the creation of one flowing line. This line basically represents the average price within a given time frame. Volatility is smoothed out by the moving average line. This makes it easier to spot points of convergence and divergence on a well-established price trend.

Traders and investors prefer to see moving averages that trend upwards. They also prefer to have a stock's current price closing higher than the trailing average. This way, a trader or investor will be confident that the stock is headed in the right direction.

There is a clear red line that cuts across the volume bars. This is another moving average line, specifically the 50-day moving average. The line is derived by adding together the total of volumes traded in the past 50 days and then divide this by 50.

Comparing Stock Market Indexes

Investors use stock market indexes as a general measure of how the stocks or securities markets are faring on any given day. Let us assume that you are a trader, and your portfolio of securities is headed south. If the indices are also on a downward trend, then you can assume that there are lethargy and pessimism in the general economy.

However, if your portfolio is underperforming while the indices are on an upward trend, then you may wish to reconsider some of your investments. The health of the stock market is often measured using different market indices. When the economy is faring well, then the indices will rise. However, when the economy is depressed, then the markets will follow suit and the indices will be on a downward trend.

Two Popular Stock Market Indices

The two best known and most popular stock market indices are the Standard and Poor's 500 Index and the Dow Jones Industrial Average – DJIA. These two indices are popularly known as the securities market's benchmark. They are both important because they provide an indication of the wellbeing of the securities market. They also give traders and investors a historical basis that they can rely on to gain invaluable insights into the on-goings at the markets and also derive useful data.

The DJIA is made up of 30 US companies with large market capitalization. The S&P 500 represents 500 major firms that have huge market capitalization and are usually selected by a committee. We also have the NASDAQ 100. This index consists of both US and international large-cap firms but not any from the financial services sector.

Process of Conducting the Indexes Comparison

1. Determine the indices you wish to compare.
We have observed that there are 2 major indices as well as NASDAQ. Each of the indices differently

fares—hence, one may be down, while the others are up, and so on.

2. Note that there are other smaller indices.
There are numerous types of stocks indices across different markets. Some of the smaller ones include the Dow Jones Transport Average. Some are industry-specific so choose carefully the indices you wish to compare.

3. Choose your preferred time frame.
Basically, the components of a particular index are likely to change based on a number of factors. The price is also likely to change so consider the time frame that you are interested in.

4. Check out charting sites and compare prices.
There are websites that contain the prices of different stocks and shares. Useful websites that you can visit include Yahoo Finance. You will get the information that you need regarding specific stock market indices. Other websites where you can find charts with indices include www.smartmoney.com, www.fool.com, and www.bigchart.com. Once you get to the charts, find

the advanced chart feature for one index then enter the symbol of the index you wish to compare.

Candlestick Patterns

Traders also use candlestick patterns as technical indicators. We can have a single candlestick or a combination of two or even three. Candlesticks are widely used indicators that enable us to observe potential trend reversals and market direction changes.

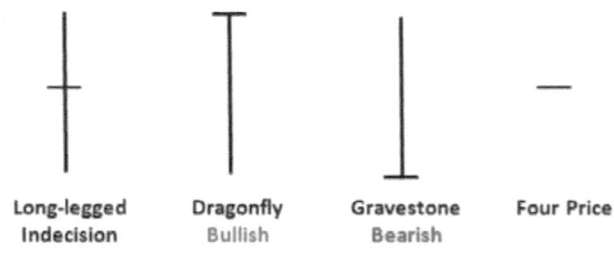

| Long-legged Indecision | Dragonfly Bullish | Gravestone Bearish | Four Price |

Candlesticks are formed based on the price action in a given period of time. For instance, if we have a candlestick based out of a 5-minute chart, then it will demonstrate the price action for the specific 5-minute period. The same is true for the 1-hour and even 4-hour time periods.

Chapter 8: Swing Trading Strategies

Swing traders use strategies that focus on making smaller but frequent gains within brief trading periods and exiting trades quickly. While the profits are smaller, when done consistently over a period of time, they do add up to a pretty decent amount. The annual returns of swing trading are rather attractive compared to investing and to other forms of trading.

Swing Trading Strategies

Most swing traders have a modest strategy which, over time, becomes a pretty lucrative one. Think about investors who wish to earn 12% - 15% on the markets annually. Swing traders target amounts between 5% and 10% each month which, when compounded throughout the year, can add up to a pretty lucrative amount.

Swing traders have to factor in losses as well. First of all, the mean time for a swing trade is usually between 5 and 10 days even though some last much longer. In this time, you could incur some losses. Therefore, keep losses at a minimum. This is achieved by maintaining stop-loss points at 2% - 3% even though others allow losses of up to 7% and 8%. Keeping losses to a minimum is crucial for long-term profitability. Your profit to loss ratio should not be lower than 3:1.

Best Swing Trading Strategies

There are various swing trading strategies that are popularly used by traders. These have different variations and feature setups that have been tried and tested over the years. It is advisable to learn more about swing trading strategies then learning two or three before eventually finding one that suits you perfectly.

1. Breakouts Strategy

One of the most popular swing trading strategies is breakouts. This strategy happens when a trader assumes a position very early during the upward trend. As a trader, you need to be extremely alert to any happenings, changes, and movements in the markets. Therefore, if you are to apply this strategy, then you should be extremely fast and identify the trend as early as possible.

As a trader, you will first monitor this stock and watch out for the necessary volatility, and momentum. It should also break any significant points of resistance or support. This means it fits perfectly within a preferred price range. This makes it easy to enter a trade. Using this approach, support, volume, and resistance will be crucial. However, there could be other factors to watch out for such as any catalysts and so on.

A breakout often happens to be a price that extends outside predefined support and resistance levels at high volumes. In such a situation, a day trader enters the market in a short position if the stock falls below support level or enters a long position if the stock price rises above the resistance.

This kind of strategy is often the starting point of expansions in volatility and major price moves. If a trader is able to manage this strategy properly, the risks are often very limited, yet profits will be maximized.

Two Types of Breakouts

Before proceeding further, you need to understand that there are two types of breakouts. These are the;

- ☐ Swing high and swing low breakouts
- ☐ Support and resistance breakouts

As a day trader, if you are looking to enter a market after the price has moved beyond a pre-defined range, then you will be breaking out. Any breakout that occurs has to be accompanied by volume.

Also, a true breakout is always accompanied by a bold, huge, candle chart formation that closes out way above the support resistance level. Therefore, as a rule of thumb, the bigger the breakout candle, the better the breakout.

2. Breakdown Strategy

This strategy is actually the direct opposite of the breakout strategy. In this instance, the price of the stock moves lower than a set support level. Using the breakdown strategy, you will keep monitoring all the fundamentals even as the chart indicates imminent downtrend towards lower price action.

You need to come up with a swing trading chart. If this chart is to be profitable, then it should contain a couple of things. One of these is the moving average or MA. There are different kinds of moving averages, such as the simple moving average, SMA, and the exponential moving average, EMA. Other crucial factors that should constitute the chart include volatility, short interest, and float.

3. Range Expansion Strategy

What is a range expansion? Range expansion can be defined as a gradual lengthening or expansion of the price bars of a particular stock with time. In this case, the high and low ranges get wider, which is usually an indication of a continuation pattern.

Process of Swing Trading a Range Expansion

It is an established fact that stocks spend a significant amount of time within a certain range. However, they do occasionally move out of range into what is known as a momentum burst. Momentum bursts often last between 3 and 5 days before returning back to the range. This is a very common phenomenon of most stocks.

The momentum burst of 3 to 5 days typically has a magnitude of 8 – 40%. Stocks with a lower price sometimes have the most spectacular price moves ever. Momentum bursts of this nature all begin with range expansion. If you scan the charts on a daily basis, then you are likely to come across numerous momentum bursts. However, you need to note that not every single momentum is worth buying into.

It is now quite clear that the most important factor is to understand the momentum bursts. All stocks progress with regular momentum bursts that occur mostly during a bullish run. Stocks can gain between 8% and 20% during such bursts, which sometimes may not have a clear driver. This run tends to last only

3 to 5 days. Lower-priced stocks tend to gain even higher percentages.

This is not a new phenomenon and has been observed during bull market runs for over 100 years. Traders have developed breakout setups mostly because they are predictable and offer very attractive risk versus rewards outcomes.

4. The Pullback Strategy

Low Risk and High Reward

As a trader, you know that there are only two ways to enter a trade. You can only enter on a breakout or a pullback. Understanding this fact is crucial, especially for day traders.

How do you define a pullback? A pullback can be defined as a situation where the price moves against an underlying trend temporarily. When a stock is on an upward trend, then a pullback is a move that is lower than the trend. However, when the trend is downwards, then the pullback trends higher.

In essence, a pullback describes security's falling back price after rising to a peak. Traders often view these price movements as short-term reversals of the current trend, which signals a temporary pause in the ascending momentum.

Pullbacks: By their very own nature, pullbacks always generate a variety of different trading opportunities after a trend moves lower or higher. Profiting through this classic strategy is not as easy as it sounds. For instance, you may invest in a security or sell short into resistance, and these trends can continue so that your losses are considerable. Alternatively, your security or stock could just sit there and waste away, even as you miss out on many other opportunities.

There are certain skills you need if you are to earn decent profits with the pullback strategy. For instance, how aggressive should a trader be and at what point must your profits be taken? When is it time to pull out? Basically, these and all other important aspects should be considered.

For starters, you require a strong trend on the markets such that other traders timing pullbacks get to line up right behind you. When they do, they will cause your idea to become a really profitable one. Securities that ascend to new heights or falling to new lows are capable of attaining this requirement, especially after the securities push much farther beyond the breakout level.

You will also need persistent vertical action into a trough or peak for regular profits, especially if the volumes are higher than usual mainly because this results in fast price movement once you attain the position. It is imperative that the stock in question turns a profit quickly after either bottoming or topping out but with no sizable trade range or consolidation. It is also crucial that this happens; otherwise, the intervening range is likely to oppose profitability during the resulting the subsequent rollover or bounce.

A Closer Look at Pullback Setups

Traders often view pullbacks as excellent buying opportunities once a particular stock has gone through a major price movement. For instance, a share may go through an impressive rise after a report of positive earnings only to experience a pullback when traders begin to take profit. The good earnings report largely implies that the shares will continue the upward trend.

Pullbacks often involve a stock's price shifting to a region of technical support before returning to the upward trend. Examples of technical support include the pivot point and moving average. As a trader, you should be very careful and observe these areas of support because any breakdown resulting from them could indicate a price reversal and not a pullback. Pullbacks are often referred to as consolidations or retracements by some traders.

Pullbacks Versus Price Reversals

As a trader, you need to be able to distinguish between a price pullback and a reversal. Reversals and pullbacks both involve the shifting price of a stock from an initial high. The difference is that reversals are longer term while pullbacks are often short term.

Now, most price reversals will involve a share's underlying fundamentals that cause the market to reevaluate its worth. Take for instance, a firm that reports poor earnings. This is likely to cause investors to recalculate the firm's share price. In some markets, lower demand for cars could lead to reduced demand for oil, steel, and related commodities, and this could be expected to continue in the long run. This is a typical price reversal situation.

However, when the fundamentals of a stock are not affected by the price, then this situation is simply referred to as a price pullback, which is always temporary. Traders often get a chance to collect profits in such cases after a particular stock does rally strongly. Take for instance, a company that announces a huge increase in profit earnings, causing the shares to jump by 50%. The stock may experience a brief pullback the following day due to day traders locking in their profits. However, the strong earnings report indicates that the stock will continue to rise in the long term.

In short, pullback situations are often viewed as opportunities to buy into stocks after they experience a huge price increase. The pullback should not be confused with a price reversal, which is often a long term, downward trend, and the stock fundamentals are affected. It is important to use technical analysis to determine that the pullback will remain well above key support levels in order to avoid losses.

Best Approach to Master the Pullback Technique

Pullbacks provide traders with all sorts of trading opportunities once an active trend ascends or descends. However, profiting from pullback setups is not as easy as it may sound. For instance, if you buy a stock whose price is dipping, or sell a stock at a loss, then the trend could continue such that you end up suffering even further losses. Alternatively, the stock could gather dust waiting for your next step. Fortunately, there are some favorable technical conditions that can enable a pullback to turn positive once you risk in reverse direction.

A Real-Life Example

Take Microsoft Corp shares, for instance. They trade using the ticker symbol MSFT. Now MSFT stock builds a range, for 3 months, below 42 then shortly thereafter the stock breaks out in the month of July.

The rise gets to 45.70 points then relaxes for seven days before selling off and losing almost 50% of the initial trend. It then comes into powerful support on the breakout level. By midday, the stock prints a small candlestick chart that indicates a possible reversal, and rises by more than 2 points. This can then be viewed as a typical and real-life pullback situation.

Identify the Best Entry Point

Once the pullback is in motion, you should look out for a cross-verification. Cross-verification refers to a slim price zone wherein different kinds of resistance or support queue opt for a fast price reversal and a powerful movement in the general trend of the stock.

Chances that a rollover or bounce will increase when the zone is compressed as tightly as possible and different types of support and resistance lined up as required. By using your technical analysis tools, you will easily align pullback points with a moving average like the 50-day EMA or a major Fibonacci retracement. For instance, a selloff to a breakthrough via horizontal highs that aligns with the 50-day moving average significantly improves the chances of a profitable pullback trade.

You should enter a pullback instance where the circumstances are less advantageous by considering resistance and support at levels of price activity and not thin lines and by maneuvering into opposing price levels.

Now consider another firm, Levi, which portrays a 10-month trading range and displaying resistance at 14 points. It then climbs vertically complete with a huge volume breakout as soon as a new, highly respected manager joins the firm. The news about the manager causes a large one-day gain in the share price. This then leads to a sudden pullback that finds support at the top of the range, which is now at 65% on the 50-day moving average as well as a Fibonacci retracement.

Trade on Short-Term Pullback Strategy

There are plenty of opportunities provided by short-term pullbacks. Stocks that experienced recent pullbacks on the stock markets against longer-term upward trends provided investors with excellent opportunities to buy the stocks. Take Moody's stock, for instance. It once traded at a high of $103.34 last November. This share then recouped and settled at $92. By observing the long-term trend, this could easily be thought of as a great point to enter the trade.

As a trader, you can jump in at this point, and buy the stock. Some of the prices you can opt should range between $94.40 and $94.60. Remember to include a stop loss at just below $92. Once you buy the stock, you can then sell when the price rises again to between $100.75 and $101. If you are experienced, you can hold on for much longer and hope the price gets to $104.50.

Another popular share, the MGM, attained trend line resistance in December of 2017. It then fell rather sporadically from that level, but the price started stabilizing in early January. To enter this trade favorably, go for $21.25 which is closer to the apex of the January position. You can place a cautionary stop loss above $21.80 and at $18.45. This target price is obviously higher than the low price witnessed recently at $17.25. However, the stronger reversal bars of mid-December indicate increasing buying pressure. If the price drops further below $17.25, then the next price target should be about $16.50.

Stop Loss Measures

There are about three reasons why traders lose money when trading pullbacks. It could be due to a miscalculation that results in entering a trade too early. Another reason could be that you enter at the best price, but unfortunately, the reverse trends break logical mathematics and work against you. It could also be due to the rollover aborting because your risk management strategy was not successful.

The third scenario is the easiest to manage. All you need to do as a trader is to place a trailing stop immediately behind your position once it adjusts the position to favor you. You then need to adjust whenever the profit increases. Basically, the stop that you require is directly related to the entry price you choose. Once you become a more experienced trader, it will be easier to observe that numerous pullbacks often indicate logical entry levels at various points.

For your stops to be more effective, you will need to wait longer. Also, the pullback will have to go deeper, but without affecting your technical analysis. This way, you will be able to place your stops only a couple of cents behind an important cross-verification level. With this approach, you are likely to miss excellent reversals at the intermediate levels, but you will also enjoy some of the lowest losses and biggest profits possible.

Chapter 9: The Daily Routine of a Swing Trader

Swing traders differ from investors in various ways. Investors buy shares and hold on to them for lengthy periods of time. They often hope to generate annual returns, like 10% to 20% per annum on their investments. This is a different approach from traders who enter the markets and exit after a very short while. Traders hope to make small but frequent profits in the course of a few days or weeks. Their aim is to make between 10% - 15% or more each month. This translates into big returns over time.

Swing traders use both fundamental analysis and technical analysis to determine stocks with an upward trend and with momentum. A swing trader's work includes the identification of financial instruments such as stocks that have a well-defined trend.

The aim of a swing trader is to purchase securities when the prices are low, hold the securities for a couple of days, and then exit when the prices are high. This way, they exit trades profitably, and it is the method that they use to earn their profits. It makes sense to enter trades when prices are low and then sell when the prices go up.

As a retail trader, you may be at a disadvantage compared to professional traders. Professional traders are generally more experienced, have a lot of leverage, access to more information, and pay lower commissions. However, you do have some advantages in some instances because you are not limited to the risks that you can take, size of investment, and types of trades. As a retail swing trader, you need to ensure that you have all the knowledge necessary to take full advantage of the markets.

Trading Techniques

Swing trading techniques are easy to learn. They are also straightforward and simple to demonstrate. After learning these techniques, it is advisable to put them to practice for a couple of days until you get confident enough to trade live. If your practice trades were largely successful, then trading the real markets will also likely prove to be successful.

As a swing trader, you do not have to focus your energies using complicated formulas and learning complex techniques. You also do not need to buy and hold stocks or other financial instruments like currencies. Instead, you only need your trading charts.

Beginning of the Trading Day

As a swing trader, you need to be up early before the markets open. Most traders are awake by 6.00 in the morning and start preparing for their trading day. The few moments just before the opening of the markets are crucial as you get the feel of the market.

One of the first things that you need to focus on is finding a potential trade. You should spend your time finding securities that are on a sure trend. Another thing you should focus during these early morning moments is creating a watch list of stocks and securities. Also, check out all your other positions.

Current News and Developments

You should take time in the morning to catch up with the latest developments and news, especially those that directly impact businesses. One of the best sources of financial and business news is CNBC, which is a cable news channel. Another great source of market information is the website www.marketwatch.com. This is an informative website that provides the latest and most reliable market news.

As a swing trader, you need to be on the lookout for three things in the news. These are different sentiments in various market sectors, current news reports such as earnings reports, and the overall market outlook. Are there sectors that are in the news? Is the news considered good or bad? What significant thing is happening in other sectors? If something significant or of concern happens, then you are likely to come across it in the news.

Identifying Potential Trades

So how do you find trades that you'd be interested in? As a swing trader, you may want to find a catalyst. A fundamental catalyst will enable you to enter a trade with sufficient momentum. Then all you will need is technical analysis to confirm your exit and profit points.

1. Special Opportunities

There are different ways of entering the market. One of these is to find a great opportunity with so much potential. Great opportunities can be found through companies planning an IPO, those ready to file for bankruptcy, situations of takeovers, buyouts, insider buying, mergers, acquisitions, and restructuring. These and other similar events provide excellent trading opportunities, especially for swing traders.

To find these opportunities, you need to check out the SEC website or filings from companies. Certain forms such as 13-D and S-4 contain all the relevant information that you need. You can also subscribe to the website www.SECFilings.com so as to receive notifications whenever companies file reports. While these opportunities carry some inherent risks, the possible rewards are too great to ignore.

2. Sector or Industry Opportunities

Apart from the rare opportunities, we also have opportunities that are specific to a given sector. These are opportunities that you will find on certain websites regarding sectors whose performance is well above average. For instance, we can determine that sectors such as energy are doing exceptionally well by observing energy ETFs. There are certain sectors that pose a high risk but have high returns and can be very profitable.

3. Chart Breaks

We can also rely on chart breaks to find opportunity. Chart breaks are especially suitable for swing traders.

Chart breaks are really stocks or securities that have been traded so heavily such that they are very close to major resistance or support levels. As a swing trader, you will search for opportunities out there by identifying patterns indicating breakdowns or breakouts.

These identifying patterns can be Gann or Fibonacci levels, Wolfe Waves, channels, and triangles. However, please note that these chart breaks are only useful when there is huge interest in the stock. This way, you can easily enter and exit trades. Therefore, whenever you note this chart breaks, you should also focus on factors such as price and volumes.

Securities Watch List

One of the things that you really should embark on is building a list of stocks or other securities to watch closely. The stocks that should constitute this list include those with a great chance at high volumes and upward price movement. It should also include stocks with a major catalyst.

Checking Your Current Positions

It is important to keep tabs on your current positions. You probably have other trades so take a look at these and see if there is anything needed on your part. This is something that you should focus on early before the trading day begins. You should review these positions with the benefit of foresight based on the information obtained from news sources and online sites. See if any news items will affect your current positions.

Checking this out is pretty easy and straight forward. All that you need to do is to enter the stock symbol into websites such as www.news.google.com. This will reveal plenty of essential information that you need to be successful. Should you come across any material information that can directly affect your trades, then consider what you should do, such as adjusting the different points like take profit and stop loss.

Market Hours

Now that the markets are open, it is time to get busy as a trader. During this time, you will mostly be trading and watching your screen. Check the market makers of the day and also be aware of any fake bids and asks.

Find a viable trade and apply all the skills and knowledge you have acquired to identify entry and exit points. There are plenty of techniques you can apply to arrive at these points. Think about Fibonacci extensions, for example. These can help you identify entry and exit points; you can also use price by volume and resistance levels.

As the trading day proceeds, you may need to make certain adjustments to your positions. These adjustments will depend on a number of factors. However, it is not advisable to adjust positions once you enter a trade, especially if you are planning on taking on additional risks. If you have to make adjustments, then it is better to focus more on adjusting the take profit points and stop loss levels.

After Hours

Most swing traders are largely inactive after the normal trading day is over. At this point in time, the market is not liquid at all and the available spread not suitable to enter any trades. Therefore, take this time to do some evaluation of your earlier trades and your positions. Examine your trades and see where you could do better. Focus on any open positions you may have and consider all material events that could have some effect on your positions.

Summary

To be an efficient trader, you need to have a routine. You should learn to wake up early before the beginning of the trading day and to get prepared. You also need to automate as many processes as possible. The crucial step is learning how to set up your workstation and your trading computer. Doing this ensures that you are totally ready for the trading day.

As a trader, you really need to learn how to separate charting from trading. There needs to be a different platform for charting, and in our case, www.tradingview.com comes highly recommended. It is just when you are ready to begin trading that you will log onto your trading platform.

There is a good reason for this. If you use the same platform for both charting and trading, you may fall into the trap of impulse decision. You will clearly view your orders right in front of your face. This will create a sense of panic and urgency, and you may do things in a hurry. When they are on different platforms, you create a thin layer that prevents impulsive action.

It is advisable to learn how to use templates a lot more effectively. This helps especially with the charting. Charting becomes an extremely effective and efficient process when you come up with different templates with varying colors. For instance, you can come up with a different color for resistance and support levels and other tools. The next time that you trade, it will be easy to track each tool individually based on its color code.

Also, remember to come with relevant alerts. Some traders prefer using multiple screens in order to monitor multiple developments at the same time. Instead of multiple screens, you can choose to create specific alerts so that should something relevant occur somewhere, then you will get to hear about it on time.

Alerts are crucial and will ensure that you get to find out when there is a price movement and so on.

You can use the weekends to plan the coming trading week. You can do this without the worry or concern of active markets. You can also take the time to come up with different trading strategies and styles that can help you attain your trading goals.

Think up of different situations that can arise as you trade and then come up with suitable solutions for each. This way, should any situation happen in the course of the trading week then you will be well prepared to handle it. Sometimes, though, you may feel the need to use a trading template already designed. These can be found online and are easy to download. However, you can also come up with your own trading plan and strategy to implement. In brief, you should always enter a trade with a plan in hand. This means that you should plan your trade and then trade your plan.

Conclusion

Thank you for making it through to the end of this book! Let's hope it was informative and able to provide you with all of the tools you need to achieve your goals—whatever they may be.

The next step is to begin putting everything you have learned to practice. Learning all the theory about swing trading is great, but you also have to learn how to apply this theory in a practical manner. The more effort and practice you put, the better you get as a trader.

Remember to try out different trading styles and strategies until you find one that suits your personality and is right for you. A good trader never puts all his money on one trade. You should always have different trades in place, which you will keep monitoring. If you can keep your emotions out of your trades, then you will eventually become a successful trader.

Finally, if you found this book useful in any way, a review on Amazon is always appreciated!

www.ingramcontent.com/pod-product-compliance
Lightning Source LLC
Chambersburg PA
CBHW020908180526
45163CB00007B/2664